NEW FOOD

CONTEMPORARY RECIPES, FASHIONABLE INGREDIENTS

Benjamin Lewis

All rights reserved
Copyright © 2008 by Hollander and Hechsher

Published in the United States by Hollander and Hechsher, New York.

Lewis, Benjamin., 1973-
New Food – Contemporary Recipes, Fashionable
Ingredients / Benjamin Lewis
100 p.
Hollander and Hechsher

ISBN: 978-0-9670029-1-0
1. Cookery, American. I. Lewis, Benjamin II. Title.
LLCN: 2008921162 2008
TX715

This book may not be reproduced in whole or in part or transmitted in any form or by any means, electronic or mechanical, including photocopying, recording, or by any information storage and retrieval system, without permission in writing from the publisher Hollander and Hechsher.

Hollander and Hechsher
CommentsForBen@NewFoodCookbook.com
The New Food World Wide Web Site address is
http://www.NewFoodCookbook.com

INTRODUCTION

Hundreds of years ago, Europeans were introduced to a variety of New World foods like tomatoes, potatoes and corn. They were distrusted, rejected and scorned by many, but ultimately enjoyed by a few intrepid gourmands. By the 20th century, these ingredients have become staples of world cuisine.

Imagine the first Italian putting together noodles (from Asia) with tomato sauce (from the New World), creating a new benchmark. Embracing the unknown can yield delicious results.

Have you ever seen some strange new vegetable in the supermarket, but didn't know what to do with it? Are you a caterer or professional chef looking to differentiate yourself? Are you sick of cooking the same old things? Looking for a recipe to impress your friends? Feel like trying something completely different?

Welcome to the continuing quest for new food!

The focus of each chapter is a new type of food that is now more readily available. New foods can be an ancient food rediscovered or a newly created hybrid. New foods can also be a unique ingredient only recently cultivated for mass consumption, or foods that have only recently begun to be imported on a large scale.

For example, there is increasing interest in foods with anthocyanin pigments, an antioxidant, because of possible health benefits and anti-aging properties. Anthocyanin pigments are a common natural occurrence in vegetables. These pigments range in color depending on the level of acidity in the food: red in acidic conditions such as blood oranges, and deep blue in less acidic conditions, such as blue potatoes.

Of all the new, obscure, curious and strange looking foods in this book, not a single one is the result of genetic engineering. But some of these foods are the result of selective breeding, intentional hybridizing and spontaneous mutation. That is, evolution.

Each recipe is meant to highlight the unique attributes of a particular food. The recipes focus on exploring exciting new flavors, smells, textures and colors.

I hope you enjoy preparing and eating these new foods as much as I do!

06 Citrus
- Ugli Baby Salad **8**
- Cara Cara Orange Fennel Salad **8**
- Yuzu Green Beans **11**
- Duck with Blood Orange Sauce **11**
- Pan Fried Sole with Yuzu Wasabi Butter **12**
- Maple Glazed Salmon with Szechuan Pepper **13**
- 10 Minute Chicken in Meyer Lemon Rosemary Sauce **15**
- Meyer Lemon Tart **15**
- Blood Orange Cake **16**

18 Squash
- Heirloom Squash and Chestnut Soup **20**
- Perfect Roasted Heirloom Winter Squash **20**
- Chayote Salad **21**
- Heirloom Squash Tempura with Mint Chutney Dipping Sauce **23**
- Heirloom Squash and Shiitake Mushrooms Risotto **24**
- Poached Salmon with Chayote and Fennel **25**

26 Colored Cauliflower
- Orange and Purple Cauliflower Cheese Soup **28**
- Romanesco Cauliflower Pasta **29**
- Colored Cauliflower with Garlic Aioli **31**
- Cauliflower Goat Cheese Terrine **32**
- Roasted Colored Cauliflower **33**

34 Noodles
- Cold Soba with Dipping Sauce **36**
- Udon Soup **36**
- Teriyaki Chicken with Crispy Soba Noodles **39**
- Saifun Stir Fry **40**
- Fried Saifun Spaghetti Bruschetta Appetizer **41**
- Jap Chae **43**

44 Greens
- Microgreens in Tiny Parmesan Bowls **46**
- Microgreens on Fried Goat Cheese Medallions **46**
- Cucumber Salad with Feta and Shiso **47**
- Sautéed Pea Shoots with Baby Carrots and Spring Garlic **48**
- Fruit Macerated with Shiso and Sweet Wine **49**
- Snow Pea Sprout and Radish Salad **49**

50 Root Vegetables
- Colored Carrot "Fettuccini" with Tarragon Pesto **52**
- White Carrot Ginger Soup with Chervil and Crispy Prosciutto **53**
- Golden Borscht with Goji Berries and Sour Cream **53**
- Scalloped Blue Potatoes with Blue Cheese **55**
- Celeriac Soup with Leeks and Bacon **56**
- Purple Carrot Cake alla Romanesca **57**

58 Heritage Meats & Farm Raised Game
- Lomo Olive Bites **60**
- Silkie Blue-Black Chicken with Silky Garlic **60**
- Squab Pilaf **63**
- Roasted Heritage Berkshire Pork Chops with Apple Pan Sauce **64**
- Ibérico de Bellota in Fettucinni **66**
- Roast Pheasant with Cumberland Sauce **67**
- Goat Kebabs **67**

68 Pomes
- Apple Poached Chicken **71**
- Asian Pear Endive Salad **72**
- Pan Roasted Pork Tenderloin with Quince **73**
- Papplequatince **74**
- Turkey Breast with Spicy Ginger-Quince Chutney **76**
- Heirloom Apple Pie **77**

78 Exotic Fruits
- Açaí Surfer Breakfast Parfait **80**
- Horny Bellini Cocktail **80**
- Guava on Endive with Goat Cheese and Pine Nuts **81**
- Pepino Prosciutto Panini **82**
- Pan Roasted Mahi Mahi with Passion Fruit **82**
- Lamb Chops with Cactus Pear Sauce **83**

84 Heirloom Tomatoes
- Heirloom Tomato Tabouli Salad **86**
- Heirloom Tomato Goat Cheese Toasts **87**
- Wild Striped Bass with Heirloom Cherry Tomatoes in Paper **88**
- Chorizo with Colored Grape Tomatoes and Saffron Rice **90**
- Heirloom Tomato Mozzarella Basil Orecchiette **91**

92 Ancient Grains
- Quinoa Granola **94**
- Lamb Mushroom Bulgur Soup **95**
- Ancient Grain and Rice Pilaf **95**
- Black Rice Pudding **96**
- Bhutanese Red Chestnut Rice **96**
- Amaranth Salad **98**

Citrus

Blood Oranges
- **Also known as:** varieties include Tarocco, Sanguinello and Moro
- **Origin and cultivation:** found as a spontaneous mutation in Sicily around the end of the 19th century; Sicily is still a major grower and, in the US, they are grown in California and Texas
- **Availability:** from winter to spring
- **Appearance:** juice really looks (and stains) like blood; color is from anthocyanin pigments which also color grapes, raspberries, blackberries and cherries
- **Flavor:** like an orange with a hint of raspberry
- **Trivia:** if blood oranges were domesticated before orange oranges, then the word "orange" could have referred to the color red

Red Naval Oranges
- **Also known as:** Cara Cara or Pink Naval
- **Origin and cultivation:** spontaneous mutation of a Washington naval orange discovered in 1976 at Hacienda Cara Cara in Venezuela, then introduced to Florida and California
- **Availability:** from winter to spring
- **Appearance:** resembles the salmon color in a pink grapefruit
- **Flavor:** like an orange with a hint of pink grapefruit
- **Trivia:** color is primarily from lycopene, a carotenoid pigment which is the same thing that colors pink grapefruit, tomatoes and watermelon

Ugli
- **Also known as:** Unique or Uniq
- **Origin and cultivation:** spontaneous hybrid of pomelo or grapefruit and tangerine, and possibly also some Seville orange; native to Jamaica; first bred in the early 1900s
- **Availability:** from late fall to summer
- **Appearance:** very ugly on the outside, with colors ranging from green to yellow and orange
- **Flavor:** yellow fruit is sweet, sour, very juicy and tastes like a mix of tangerine and grapefruit
- **Trivia:** Ugli is the trademarked name while Uniq is the generic name

Meyer Lemon

- **Origin and cultivation:** brought from China to the U.S. in 1908 by Frank Meyer; cross between lemon and a mandarin or orange
- **Availability:** from late fall to spring
- **Appearance:** looks like a rounder lemon with a smoother skin
- **Flavor:** less sour than a regular lemon with a sweet orange smell
- **Trivia:** highly prized in California and Florida where they are often grown in backyards

Yuzu

- **Also known as:** Japanese Citron or Yuja in Korea
- **Origin and cultivation:** a wild fruit in Tibet and China, was brought to Japan in around 1,000 AD; rarely found outside of Japan until recently; hybrid between mandarin and a primitive citrus called ichang papeda
- **Availability:** fall
- **Appearance:** can be yellow or green
- **Flavor:** zest has a unique fragrance unlike most other citruses
- **Trivia:** in Japan, during the winter, people will put a whole Yuzu into their bath water to create therapeutic aromas

Szechuan Pepper

- **Also known as:** Sichuan Pepper, Chinese Pepper, Japanese Pepper, Chinese Prickly Ash, Fagara, Sansho, Timur or Indonesian Lemon Pepper
- **Origin and cultivation:** the outer pod of a small fruit that has no relation to black pepper; in the citrus family but in a distinct genus from other citrus fruits such as oranges and limes
- **Availability:** year-round at stores that sell specialty spices
- **Appearance:** powdered, or in whole form that looks like little red-black split pods
- **Flavor:** an intense numbing heat that is a distinct chemical from black pepper, hot peppers, mustard, horseradish and wasabi; generally added to food after it is cooked to maximize the flavor and numbing power
- **Trivia:** banned by the U.S. FDA until 2005 because imported peppercorns could carry citrus canker disease, which threatens citrus trees. The ban was lifted, provided the peppercorns are heated

CITRUS

UGLI BABY SALAD [Starter]

- 1 ugli fruit
- 2 big handfuls of baby spinach leaves
- 1 carrot
- 1/3 cup of extra virgin olive oil
- Salt and pepper

Wash and dry the baby spinach leaves.

Peel and slice the carrot finely.

Peel the ugli fruit with your hands. Cut between each membrane to release the segments. Squeeze what is left over of the ugli fruit into a measuring cup to get about a 1/4 cup of juice.

Add salt, pepper and olive oil to the juice and whisk to make the dressing. Mix everything together and serve.

Serves 2.

CARA CARA ORANGE FENNEL SALAD [Starter]

- 2 bulbs of fennel
- 3 red naval oranges
- 1/3 cup of extra virgin olive oil
- 2 tablespoons champagne vinegar
- Salt and pepper

Cut the stalks from the fennel bulbs. Cut the bulbs in half and remove the fibrous root core. Slice the bulbs and stalks very thinly. Also, chop up some of the green fronds.

Use a knife to cut off the skin from the red naval oranges, and then slice as thin as you can.

Layer the oranges on plates then add the fennel on top. Just before serving, make a vinaigrette by whisking the olive oil, vinegar, salt and pepper. Pour the dressing over the salad.

Serves 4.

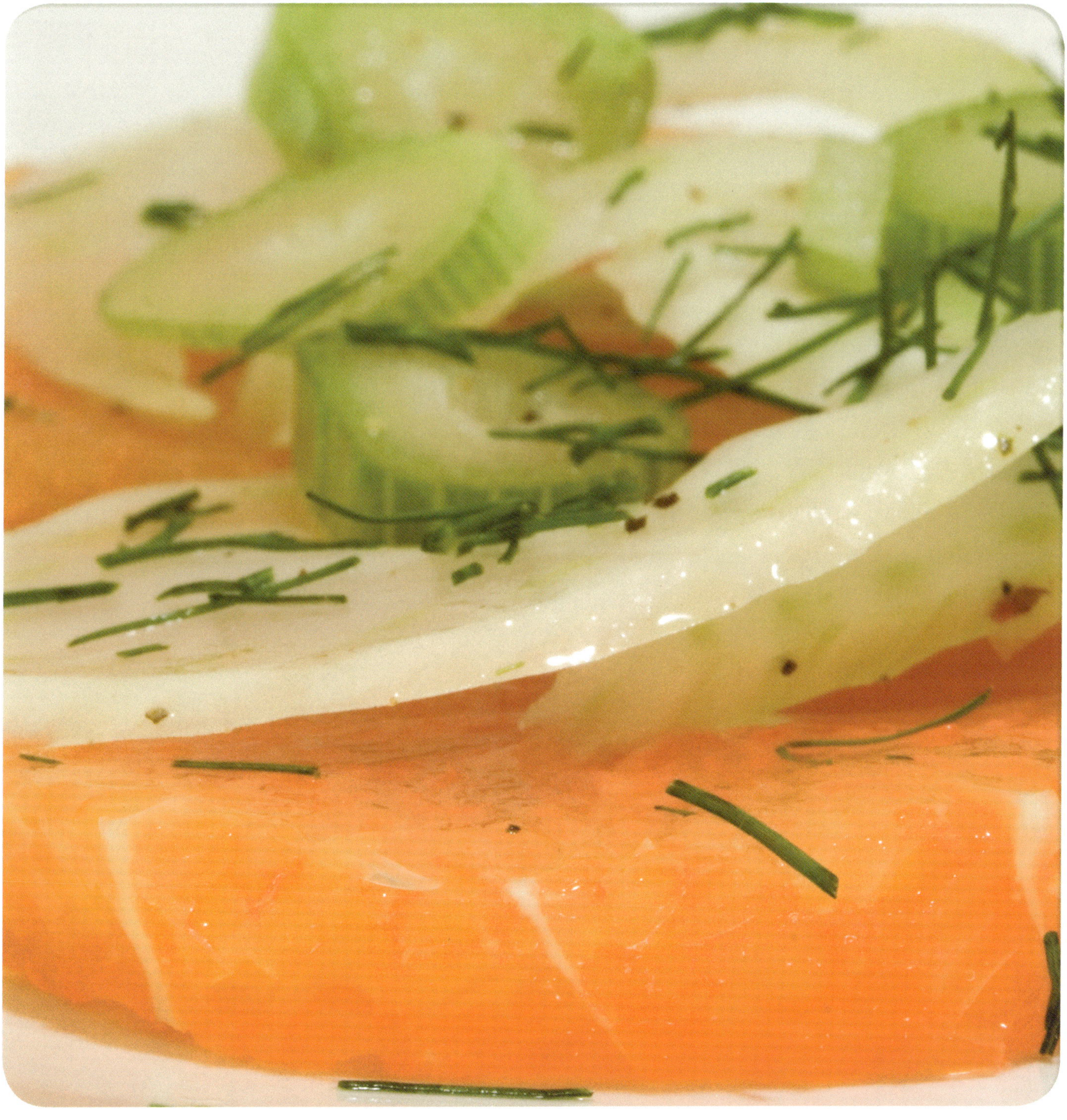

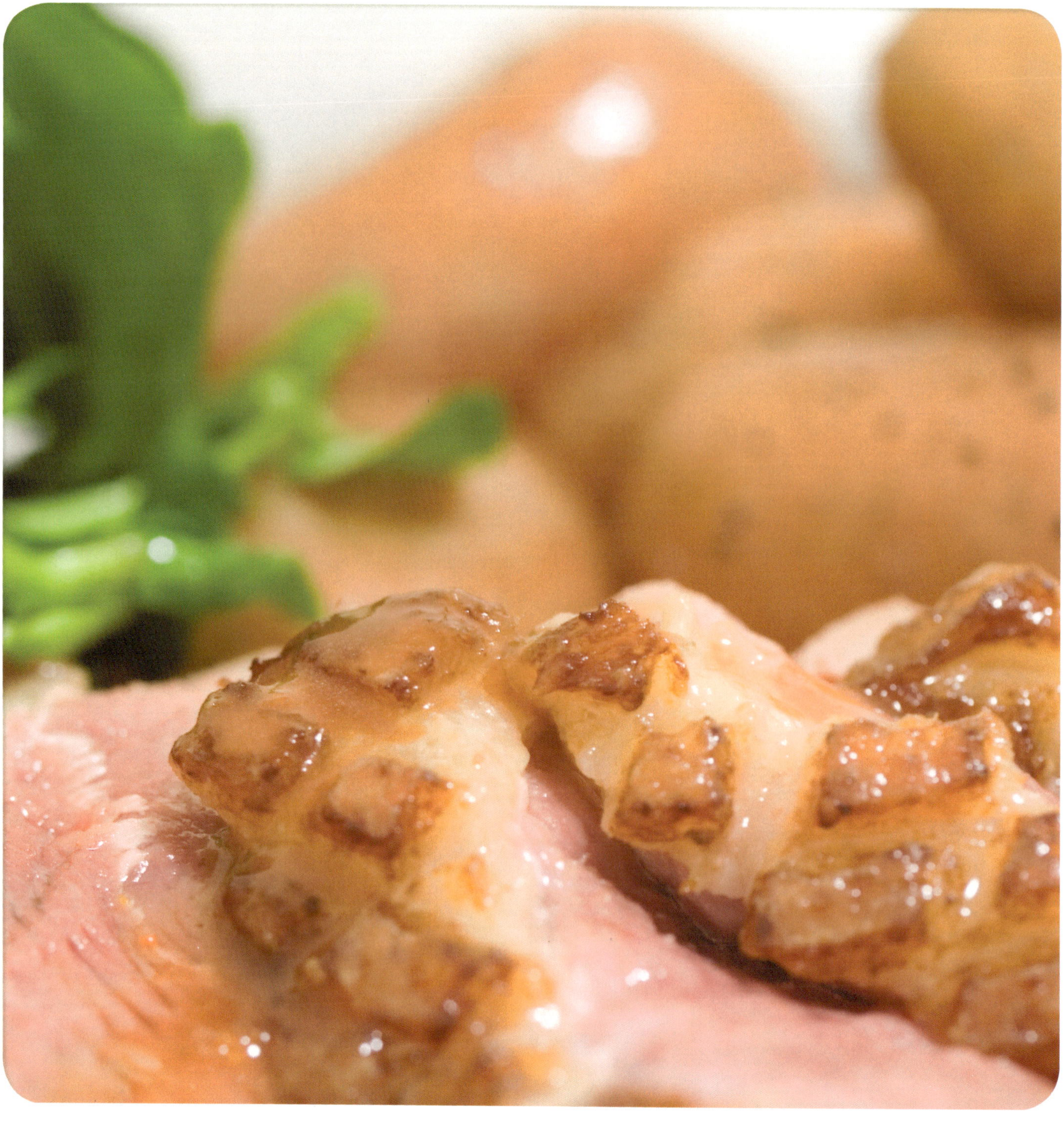

Duck with Blood Orange Sauce [Main Course]

- 1 Magret duck breast (Muscovy or other varieties will also do)
- 1/3 cup of bourbon
- Juice of 1 blood orange
- 1 teaspoon of blood orange zest, minced
- 1/4 cup of demi-glace
- 1 tablespoon of butter
- 1/4 teaspoon of cayenne pepper powder
- Salt

Score the duck's fat into 1/4 inch criss-cross marks without cutting into the meat. Sprinkle with salt.

Heat a heavy pan on medium and heat up the butter. Once the butter is foaming, put the heat on low and put the duck in fat side down. Cook on low for 12 minutes, occasionally pouring off the rendered fat. Flip and cook an additional 10 minutes until medium rare, an interior temperature of 135°F or cook longer until the USDA recommended 165°F. Remove and keep warm.

Pour off most of the fat. Add the bourbon to the pan and reduce by half. Add the demi-glace and blood orange juice, zest and cayenne pepper powder. Reduce until nice and thick, turn off the heat and season with salt.

Slice the duck and pour the sauce over the slices.

Serves 2.

Yuzu Green Beans [Side Dish]

- 1 pound of French green beans
- 1 yuzu
- 2 tablespoons of extra virgin olive oil
- Salt and pepper

First, zest the yuzu. Then, squeeze out the yuzu juice and put it along with the zest in a ramekin. Add the olive oil, salt and pepper and mix with a fork.

Clean the beans, then steam them for about 5 minutes until cooked but still crispy. Once the beans are cooked, toss with the yuzu olive oil mixture.

This can be served hot or refrigerated for up to two days and served cold.

Serves 4.

CITRUS

CITRUS

Pan Fried Sole with Yuzu Wasabi Butter [Main Course]

For yuzu butter:
- Zest of 1 yuzu, minced
- Juice from 1 yuzu
- 4 tablespoons of butter, at room temperature
- 1/2 teaspoon of wasabi powder
- Salt

For fish:
- 4 filets of lemon sole (filet of other mild fish will do equally well)
- 1/4 cup of flour
- 1 tablespoon of butter
- Salt and pepper

Put yuzu juice, yuzu zest, butter, wasabi powder and salt in a mini food processor and cream for 1 minute. Scoop out and put in cling wrap or parchment paper. Form the butter into a 1 inch diameter cylinder. Put the wrapped butter in the refrigerator for at least 1 hour to harden. Or, seal in a plastic bag and put in an ice bath for 15 minutes.

Lightly dredge the fish filets in flour, salt and pepper.

If you can't fit all the fish in the pan in one batch, then cook it in two batches.

Put 1 tablespoon of plain butter in a large pan and heat medium-high until hot. Put in the fish. Cook for 2 minutes, add another bit of butter if dry, flip and cook for 2 to 3 more minutes until done.

Slice up the hardened yuzu butter into pats, and serve on the fish.

Serves 2.

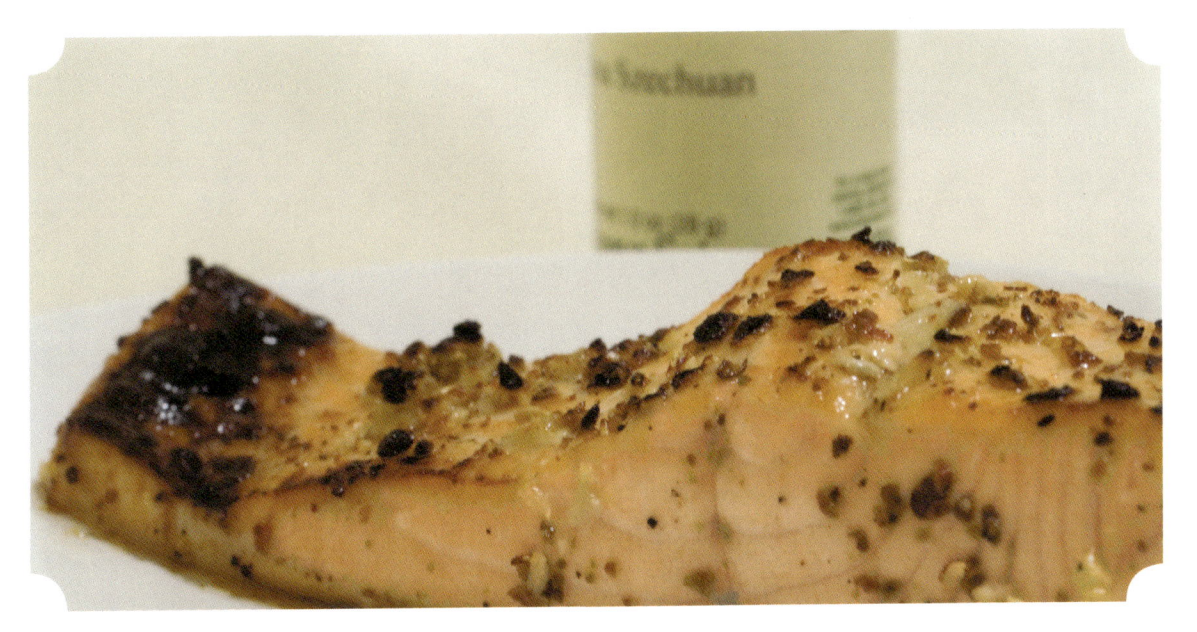

Maple Glazed Salmon with Szechuan Pepper [Main Course]

- 2 salmon filets, 1 inch thick
- 1/4 cup of maple syrup
- 1 clove garlic, minced
- Juice of a 1/4 lemon
- 1/2 teaspoon of olive oil
- 1 teaspoon of ground black pepper
- 1 teaspoon of Szechuan pepper, coarsely ground
- 1/4 teaspoon of salt

Preheat your broiler.

Mix syrup, lemon juice, garlic, salt and black pepper in a bowl. Dip the salmon in the bowl coating it well.

Put some aluminum foil in your broiling pan and grease with olive oil. Put the salmon filets on the foil skin side down and brush on any remaining syrup mixture.

Broil for 8 to 10 minutes on the second to lowest rack until flaky and done. If the fish is thicker than an inch and still not done after 12 minutes, turn off the broiler and let sit in the leftover heat for 5 more minutes. If you leave the broiler on longer than 12 minutes the syrup mixture might start burning.

Remove the fish and dust with the ground Szechuan pepper.

Serves 2.

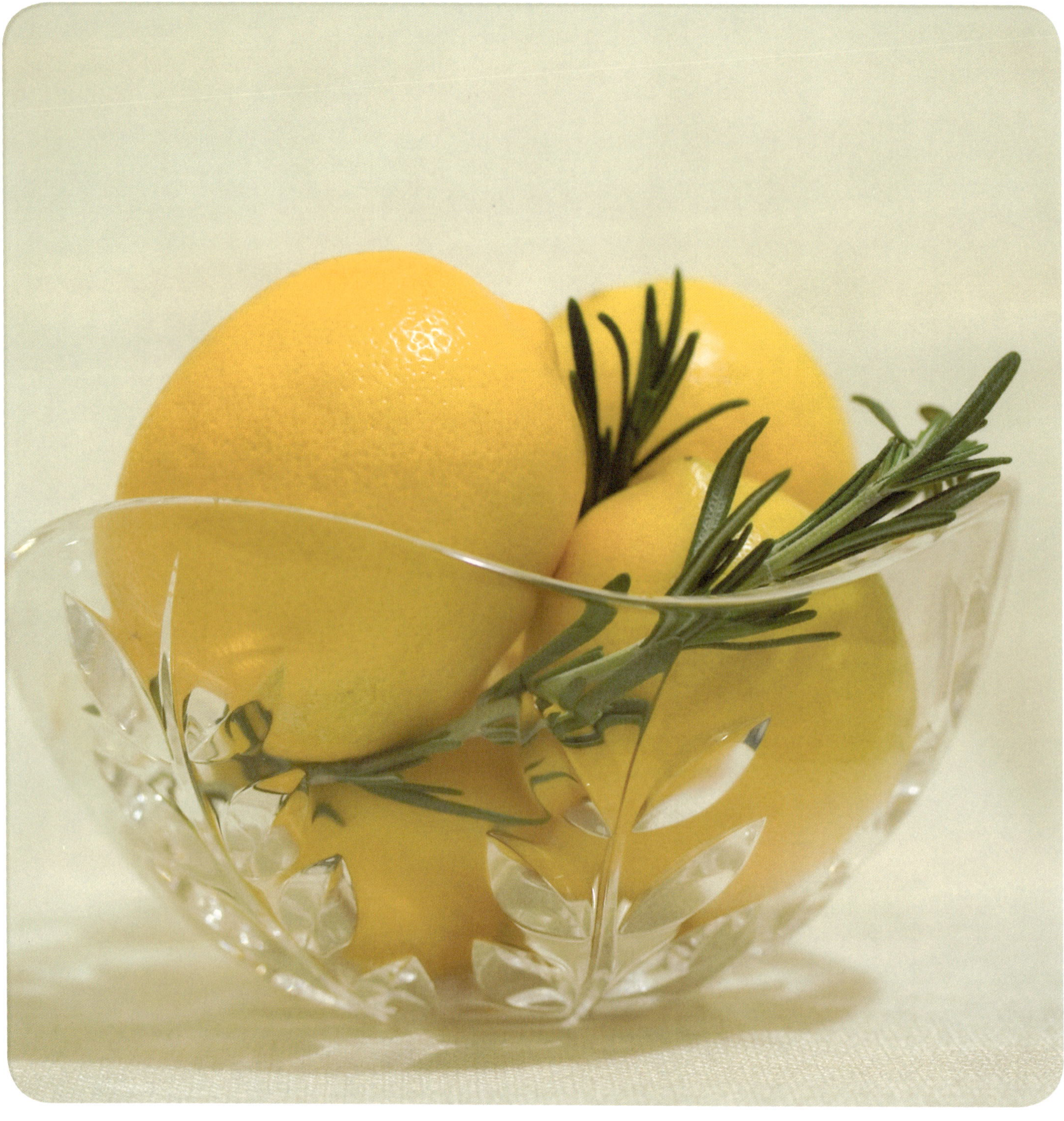

10 Minute Chicken in Meyer Lemon Rosemary Sauce [Main Course]

- 4 small chicken breasts, boneless and skinless
- 1 tablespoon of fresh rosemary, chopped
- Zest from 1 Meyer lemon, minced
- 1 tablespoon of juice from Meyer lemon
- 1 cup of demi-glace
- 2 tablespoons of butter
- 1 tablespoon of olive oil
- Salt and pepper

First, pound the chicken flat, using a heavy pan, in between 2 pieces of cling wrap sprinkled with a little water. Then, dry the chicken well with a paper towel.

Cook the chicken in two batches. Put the pan on medium-high heat and add 1 tablespoon of butter and the olive oil. Once nice and hot, add 2 pieces of chicken and cook for 3 minutes, then flip and cook for another 2 minutes or until done. Remove the chicken and keep warm. Repeat with the second batch.

In the same pan, add the demi-glace, rosemary and Meyer lemon zest. Cook on high heat for around 2 minutes, stirring up any brown bits stuck to the bottom of the pan, until it is thick and rich. Remove from the heat and add the Meyer lemon juice along with the remaining tablespoon of butter. Add salt and pepper. Add the chicken back to the pan to coat with sauce and serve.

Serves 4.

Meyer Lemon Tart [Dessert]

For the 9 inch tart shell:
- 1 1/2 cup of ground graham crackers
- 1 tablespoon of sugar
- 4 tablespoons of melted butter

For the filling:
- 3/4 cup of Meyer lemon juice (from about 3 lemons)
- 2 teaspoons of Meyer lemon rind (from about 2 of the lemons)
- 1/3 cup of sugar
- 1/4 cup of crème fraîche
- 3 eggs, yolks and whites
- 2 eggs yolks
- Pinch of salt
- Powder sugar, for sifting over the chilled tart

Preheat the oven to 350°F. Make the crust by mixing the ground graham crackers, 1 tablespoon of sugar and 3 tablespoons of melted butter. Put in a 9 inch tart pan and tamp down gently with a spoon. Put the tart pan on a cookie sheet to make maneuvering easier.

Whisk the lemon juice, lemon rind and sugar until the sugar is dissolved. Then, whisk in the crème fraîche. While mixing, add the eggs and yolks, one by one until they are blended. Pour the mixture into the tart pan.

Bake 30 minutes or until filling is set. Cool on wire rack for 1 hour to bring to room temperature. Then, chill in the refrigerator for at least 2 hours or overnight.

Sift powdered sugar over chilled tart before serving.

Serves 8.

CITRUS

CITRUS

BLOOD ORANGE CAKE [Dessert]

FOR THE CAKE:
- 1 cup of butter, at room temperature
- 1 1/2 cup of flour
- 1/4 teaspoon of baking powder
- 1 1/2 cup of sugar
- Zest of 1 blood orange, minced
- 2 tablespoons of blood orange juice
- 5 egg yolks
- 5 egg whites
- Dash of salt

FOR THE ICING:
- 1/2 cup of powdered sugar
- 2 tablespoons blood orange juice

Grease a 9 inch loaf pan with a little butter.

Preheat your oven to 300°F.

Sift the baking powder and salt into the flour in a bowl. Add 3/4 cup of the sugar. Add 1 cup of butter and use an electric mixer with beater attachments to mix it up. While continuing to mix, add the 2 tablespoons of orange juice and orange zest. Then, while mixing, add the egg yolks, one by one until they are blended.

In another bowl, using the electric mixer with a whisk attachment, beat the egg whites until stiff. Gently whisk in 3/4 cup of sugar.

Using a rubber spatula, fold the beaten egg whites into the first mixture.

Spoon the batter into the loaf pan and smooth out with the rubber spatula. Gently tap the pan on the counter a few times to remove any air bubbles.

Bake for 1 1/2 hours or until done. While still in the pan, cool for 30 minutes on a wire rack. Then, remove from the pan and continue cooling on a rack for another hour or two.

Make the icing by slowly adding a few drops of blood orange juice to the powdered sugar, mixing until it looks like icing. Then, ice the cake and let cool.

Serves 8.

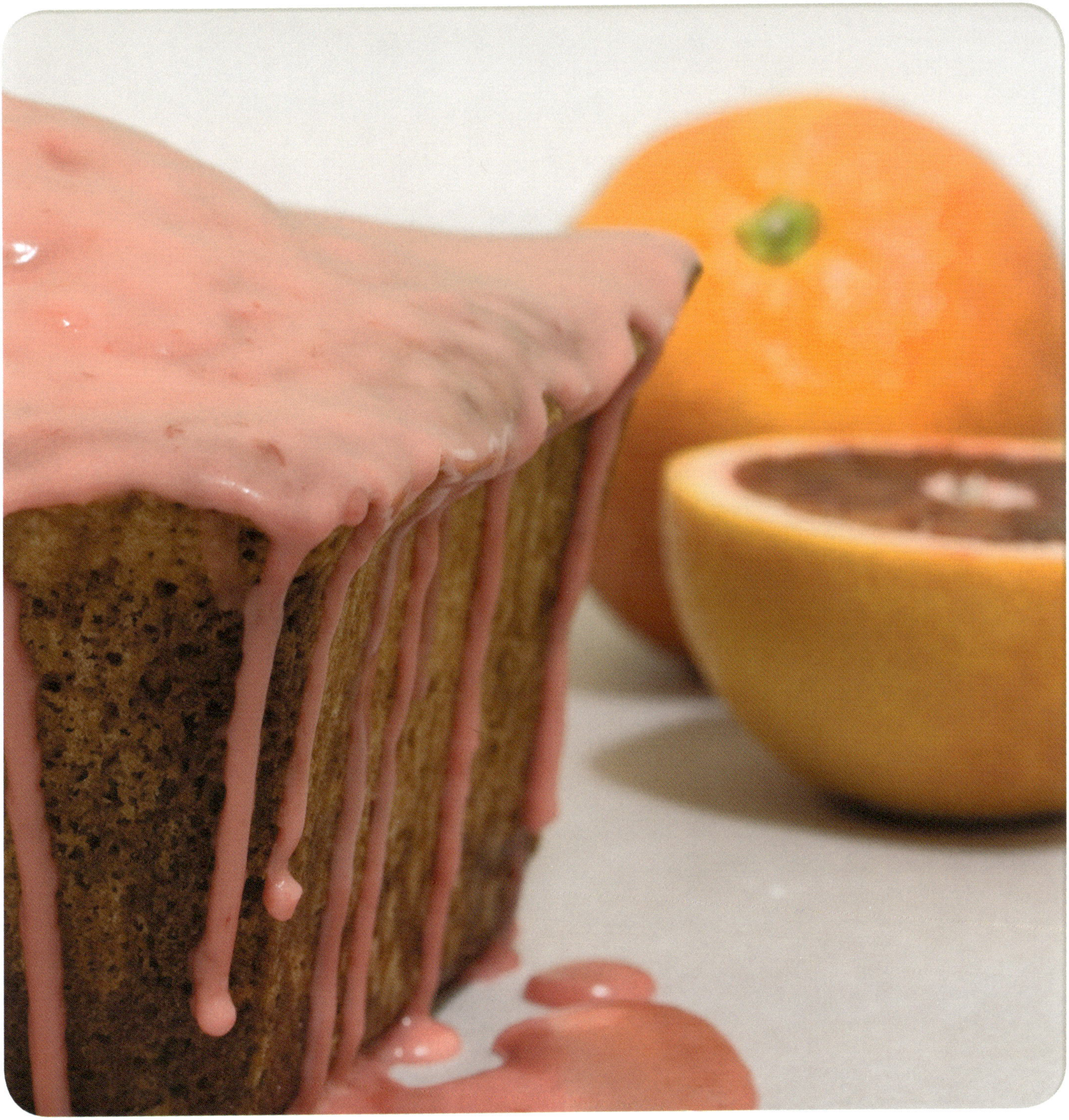

Squash

Chayote
- **Also known as:** Chayotli, Christophen, Christophine, Vegetable Pear, Mango Squash, Mirliton, Choco, Xu-xu, Zucca, Alligator Pear, Kajot, Choke, Pepineca or Buddha's Hand Squash
- **Origin and cultivation:** from Mesoamerica, popular with Aztecs and Maya; cultivated world wide, and popular in Asia as well as Central and South America
- **Availability:** found year-round especially in Latin groceries
- **Appearance:** resembles a bright green pear, with a wrinkled crevice on the bottom; can be smooth on the outside, wrinkly on the outside, or prickly
- **Flavor:** mild slightly sweet flavor with hints of cucumber and almonds; all parts are edible including the skin, seed, roots, leaves and stem
- **Trivia:** keeps its shape very well after cooked; depending on the variety, can be mildly astringent and feel slippery when raw (in that case, use rubber gloves to handle)

Heirloom winter squash
- **Also known as:** Cheese Pumpkin, Marina di Chioggia, Banana, Blue Hubbard, Sweet Meat, Red Kuri, Turban and many many more; new hybrids include Carnival, Stripetti, and Eat It All
- **Origin and cultivation:** originally from the New World, taken to Europe by Christopher Columbus
- **Availability:** fall, especially at farmers markets
- **Appearance:** varies from orange to white to blue, striped to solid, big to small, round to oval, smooth flesh to stringy
- **Flavor:** varies from pumpkin to sweet potatoes
- **Trivia:** name isn't scientific, rather a definition of a squash having a hard outer rind that can be stored through the winter

www.newfoodcookbook.com

19

HEIRLOOM SQUASH AND CHESTNUT SOUP [Starter]

- 1 heirloom winter squash (about 4 pounds)
- 10 fresh chestnuts
- 1 teaspoon of fresh ginger, minced
- 1/2 tablespoon of butter
- 1 cup of calvados
- 4 cups of chicken stock
- 1 small onion, minced
- Salt and pepper

Carefully cut an X in each chestnut with a knife. Microwave them for about 35 seconds. Let cool for at least 5 minutes and peel off the shells.

Cut the squash in half and remove the seeds. Cut off the peel and chop into 1/2 inch cubes.

In a medium pot, sauté the onion and ginger in butter for 5 minutes on low heat to soften. Add the calvados and reduce by half to remove the alcohol. Add the squash cubes, chestnuts, stock, salt and pepper. Bring to a boil and simmer for 20 minutes until the squash is tender.

Remove from heat and purée using a hand blender.

Serves 4.

PERFECT ROASTED HEIRLOOM WINTER SQUASH [Side Dish]

- 2 softball sized heirloom winter squash, such as a Carnival
- 1/4 cup of bacon drippings (or duck fat or melted butter)
- 1/2 teaspoon of freshly grated nutmeg
- Salt and pepper

Preheat your oven to 400°F.

Cut the squash in half laterally and scoop out the seeds.

Drizzle with bacon drippings, nutmeg, salt and pepper. Wrap in aluminum foil.

Put directly on baking sheet in the middle rack of the oven and bake for 30 minutes. Peel off the foil and bake for about 15 more minutes or until done.

Serves 4.

Chayote Salad [Starter]

- 2 chayote squash
- 2 tablespoons of cilantro, chopped
- 2 tablespoons of red or orange hot pepper, finely chopped
- Juice of 1 lime
- 1/3 cup of extra virgin olive oil
- Salt and pepper

Using rubber gloves, peel the chayote with a vegetable peeler. Slice in half and remove the soft seed in the middle. Dice the chayote into 1/4 inch cubes. Simmer in salted water for 10 minutes, drain, and cool down in an ice bath.

Make the dressing by whisking the lime juice, olive oil, salt and pepper.

Toss the chayote with the hot pepper, cilantro and dressing.

Serves 2.

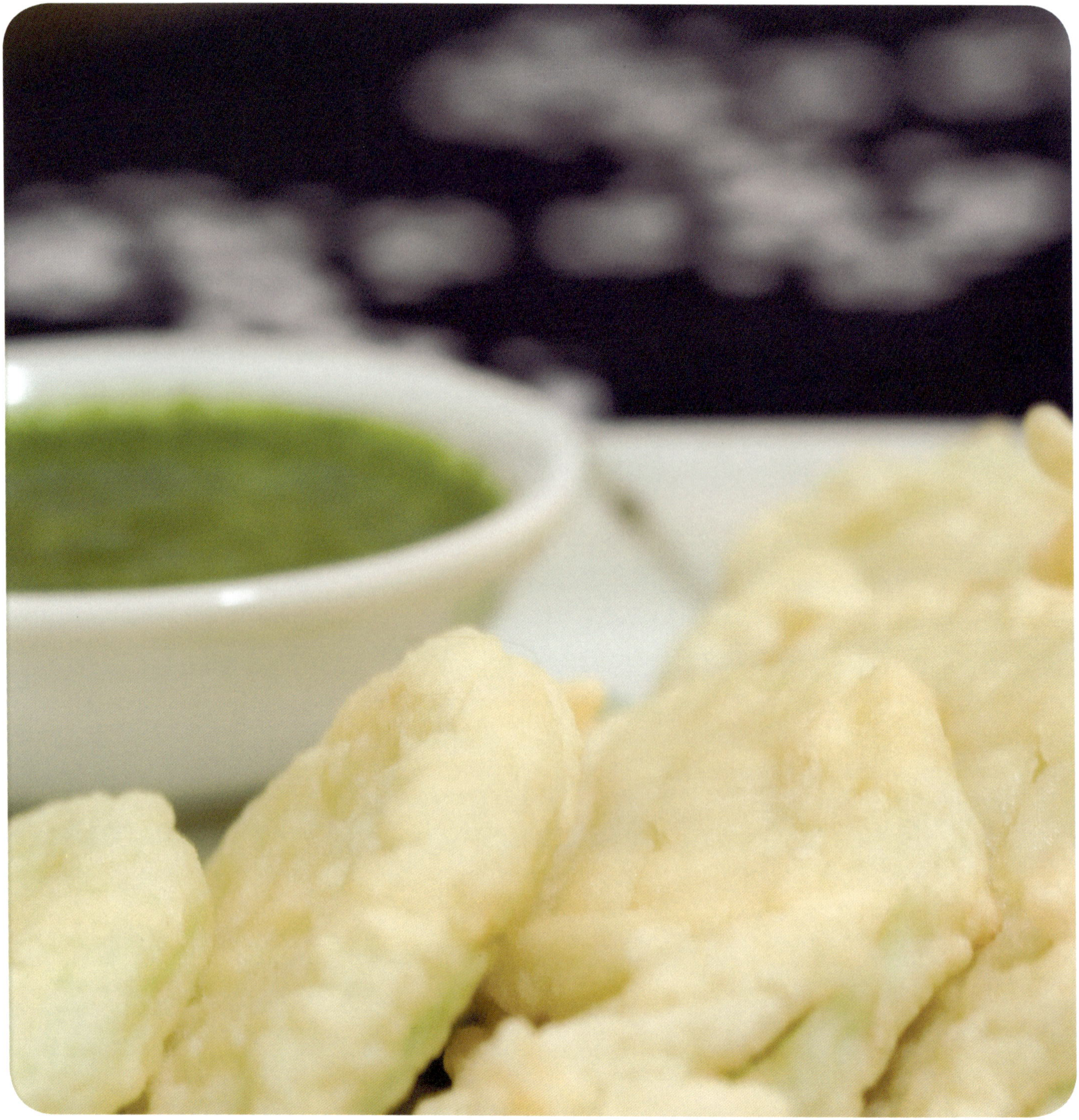

Heirloom Squash Tempura with Mint Chutney Dipping Sauce [Starter]

- 1 small heirloom winter squash (about 2 pounds)
- 1 cup of flour, sifted and cold by putting in the freezer for a bit
- 1/4 cup of flour for dusting the squash before dipping in the batter
- 1 cup of cold water for the batter
- 1 egg
- 1 cup of vegetable oil
- 1/3 cup of fresh mint leaves
- 1/3 cup of fresh cilantro leaves
- 1/2 inch piece of fresh ginger, peeled
- 1 small green chili
- 1 teaspoon of lime juice
- 1/4 cup of water for the dipping sauce
- Salt and pepper

Cut the squash in half and remove the seeds. Cut off the peel and slice into 1/4 inch thick pieces.

First, while the flour is in the freezer, make the mint chutney dipping sauce by puréeing the mint leaves, cilantro leaves, ginger, chili and lime juice. Then, add about 1/4 cup of water until it starts to look like a dipping sauce.

Start up the oil in a heavy pot or pan until 340°F. If you don't have a thermometer, then you can test the temperature with a drop of batter, which when put in, should sink about a 1/4 inch before floating to the top.

While the oil is heating up, make the batter. Beat the egg, and then add the 1 cup of cold water. Then, gently mix in the cold flour until blended.

Dust a few squash pieces with flour and shake off excess, dip in the batter, then fry for a few minutes until light brown, flipping once or twice. Drain on a wire rack. Repeat with the next batch.

Serve with the dipping sauce.

Serves 4.

www.newfoodcookbook.com

Heirloom Squash and Shiitake Mushroom Risotto
[Main Course]

- 1 heirloom winter squash (about 3 pounds)
- 10 fresh shiitake mushrooms
- 1 cup of arborio rice
- 1/2 cup of dry white wine
- 2 cups of chicken stock
- 2 tablespoons of butter
- 2 tablespoons of olive oil
- 1 teaspoon of fresh thyme
- 1 diced shallot
- Salt and pepper

First, preheat your oven to 400°F because you need to roast the squash. Take the squash and slice it in two laterally. Scoop out and discard the seeds, and then rub the squash with a tablespoon of olive oil. Put it on a roasting pan and roast for 30 to 45 minutes. It is done when the top turns light brown and it is all soft and mushy. Once done, scoop out the cooked squash, mash it up a bit, and put it in a bowl until you need it.

Dice the shallot and clean the mushrooms. Discard the tough shiitake stems then slice the tops. Chances are, you'll want to take the stems off the shiitakes because they can be a bit tough. Then, slice the mushrooms.

In a 2 quart pot, bring the stock to a simmer.

Now, in a different 4 quart pot, on medium heat, add 1 tablespoon of butter and oil. When it is good and hot, add the shallots. After a minute, add the mushrooms and thyme and cook for another 2 minutes. Then, add the rice, salt, and pepper, and stir for 1 minute.

Next, add the white wine and continue to stir, until it is almost evaporated. At that point, add enough boiling stock to cover the rice completely. Then, add the cooked squash. Keep the heat at a level so the liquid burbles briskly, but not too vigorously. Stir every minute or so and whenever the liquid drops below the rice, add more stock. If you run out of stock, start using boiling water instead. After about 15 to 20 minutes, the risotto should be done.

To finish, remove from heat and add the remaining tablespoon of butter.

Serves 2.

POACHED SALMON WITH CHAYOTE AND FENNEL [Main Course]

FOR THE SALMON:
- 4 salmon filets
- 2 chayotes
- 1 big fennel bulb
- 6 ounces of yogurt
- Zest of 1 lemon, minced

FOR THE POACHING LIQUID:
- Peels of one of the chayotes, along with both center seeds
- 1 shallot
- 1 bouquet garni (a bay leaf, sprig of fresh thyme and sprig of rosemary tied together)
- 1 cup of dry white wine
- Salt
- 1 or 2 cups of water

⚬ ⚬ ⚬ ⚬ ⚬ ⚬

Using rubber gloves peel the chayote. Cut in half and remove the seed. Reserve both the peels and seed for the poaching liquid. Slice the chayote.

To make the poaching liquid, in a wide pan (that has a lid you'll need to use later), add the chayote peels, the chayote seed, peeled shallot, bouquet garni, wine, and salt. Add the water so that the liquid is equal to the thickness of the salmon, but not so much that it will spill over when you add the salmon. Put on a lid and simmer the poaching liquid for about 20 minutes to get the flavors going.

Meanwhile, slice the fennel bulb in big chunks, reserving some of the chopped green fronds.

Put the salmon in a single layer in the poaching liquid and lower heat to just below a simmer. Pour some liquid over the fish. Add the fennel and chayote slices. Cover and continue cooking on very low heat for about 10 minutes, until the fish is firm and opaque. Carefully take out the salmon, fennel and chayote.

Make the sauce by mixing the yogurt with lemon zest and reserved chopped fennel fronds.

Put the salmon on top of the fennel and chayote. Top with the yogurt sauce.

Serves 2.

SQUASH

Colored Cauliflower

Purple

- **Origin and cultivation:** discovered as a spontaneous mutation in the 1980s, and improved through breeding in Denmark
- **Availability:** year-round
- **Appearance:** bright purple color
- **Flavor:** like regular white cauliflower
- **Trivia:** pigment is from anthocyanin pigments, which since water soluble, will wash out if cooked with too much water

Orange
- **Also known as:** Cheddar Cauliflower
- **Origin and cultivation:** discovered as a spontaneous mutation in 1970 in Canada; improved through breeding at Cornell University
- **Availability:** year-round
- **Appearance:** bright orange color
- **Flavor:** like regular white cauliflower
- **Trivia:** pigment is from beta-carotene (converts to Vitamin A once you eat it), the same as in orange carrots. If you eat a lot of orange cauliflower, or carrots, or anything else with beta-carotene every day, your skin will turn orange, a condition known as carotenemia.

Green Romanesco
- **Also known as:** Romanesco Broccoli, Pyramidenblumenkohl, Chou Romanesco or Calabrese Romanesco
- **Origin and cultivation:** a variety was cultivated around Rome and Naples in Italy and in the early 1990s, the variety was bred for larger scale cultivation
- **Availability:** year-round
- **Appearance:** green color comes from chlorophyll
- **Flavor:** this hybrid of cauliflower and broccoli, as you might guess, tastes like a mix between the two
- **Trivia:** florets occur in a fractal pattern

www.newfoodcookbook.com

COLORED CAULIFLOWER

Orange and Purple Cauliflower Cheese Soup [Starter]

- 1 head of orange cauliflower, roughly cut up
- 1 head of purple cauliflower, roughly cut up
- 4 cups of chicken stock (2 cups for each color cauliflower)
- 2 tablespoons of butter
- 4 tablespoons of flour
- 4 cups of milk
- 1 cup of grated orange cheddar cheese
- 1 cup of grated white cheddar cheese
- 1 tablespoon of chopped flat leaf parsley
- Salt and pepper

Get 3 pots, each about 3 quarts.

In 2 separate pots, bring the chicken stock to a boil. Add the cauliflower (one color per pot) and boil for 10 minutes until tender.

Meanwhile, while the cauliflower is boiling, make roux-thickened milk for both soups at the same time. In a third pot, melt 4 tablespoons of butter, then add 4 tablespoons of flour and cook for 2 minutes. Slowly add 4 cups of milk while on low heat, stirring constantly until thickened in a few minutes.

Purée the cauliflower in the chicken stock using a hand blender. Put on low heat and add half the thickened milk to each pot. Mix well. Then, add the cheese: cheddar for the orange cauliflower and white cheddar for the purple cauliflower. Stir until the cheese is melted. Add salt and pepper.

Serve in bowls and sprinkle with parsley. Gently swirl the colors together.

Serves 4.

Romanesco Cauliflower Pasta [Main Course]

- 1 head of romanesco cauliflower
- 2 shallots, minced
- 1/3 cup of dry white wine
- 1 pound of fresh linguini
- 3 tablespoons of fresh basil, finely chopped
- 1/3 pound of fresh mozzarella cheese, grated
- 2 tablespoons of olive oil
- Salt and pepper

Cut the cauliflower in half, cut out the inner core and break off the pointy florets into 1 inch pieces.

Put a large pan on medium-high heat and pour in the olive oil and heat up. Add the shallot and stir for a minute or two, then add the cauliflower. Continue to cook and stir for about 8 to 10 minutes uncovered until the florets start to brown.

Start making the pasta.

Add some salt and pepper to the cauliflower. Pour in the wine and deglaze the bottom of the pan by rubbing with a wooden spoon and stirring everything in the pan. Put the heat on low, cover and steam for about a minute until the cauliflower is tender. Add the basil.

Remove the sauce from the heat and pour over the pasta. Sprinkle with the mozzarella cheese.

Serves 4.

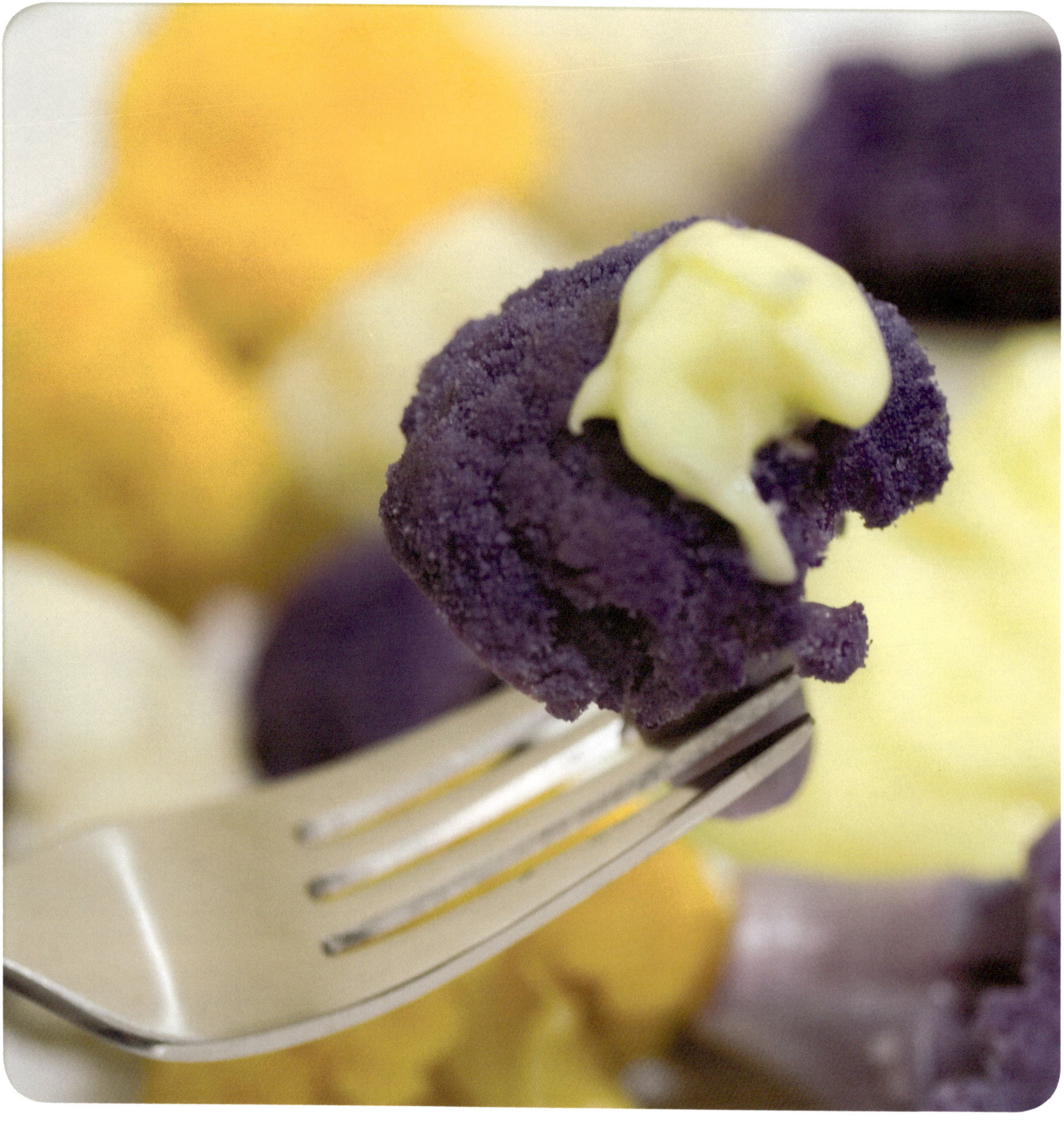

COLORED CAULIFLOWER WITH GARLIC AIOLI [Starter]

- 1 head of orange cauliflower, cut in 1 inch size pieces
- 1 head of purple cauliflower, cut in 1 inch size pieces
- 1 head of white cauliflower, cut in 1 inch size pieces
- 2 egg yolks at room temperature
- 4 cloves of garlic
- 1/2 teaspoon of salt
- 1 teaspoon of fresh lemon juice
- 1 cup of extra virgin olive oil

Continue incorporating the olive oil until you run out.

Put the aioli in a small bowl and serve with the cauliflower.

Serves 8.

You can use the cauliflower raw, in a crudité platter, or steam it for about 5 minutes until tender. Remove from heat, rinse in cold water, then put in ice water to stop from overcooking.

To make the aioli, begin by mincing and smashing the garlic as finely as possible. Put in a bowl and add the salt and egg yolk. Use an electric mixer, with whisk attachment if possible, to mix for a few seconds.

Then, while continuing to mix, add a drop or two of olive oil. Wait until it is incorporated and the eggs look just a little thicker, and then add a couple more drops of olive oil. Repeat this over and over again.

Once you've added about 1/4 cup a drop at a time, then you can start to get adventurous and start adding the oil, very gradually, in a slow stream. When about halfway done with the olive oil, add the lemon juice.

COLORED CAULIFLOWER

CAULIFLOWER GOAT CHEESE TERRINE [Starter]

- 1/2 head of orange cauliflower, cut in 1/2 inch florets
- 1/2 head of purple cauliflower, cut in 1/2 inch florets
- 12 ounces of soft goat cheese
- 4 handfuls of mixed greens
- 4 teaspoons of aged balsamic vinegar
- 1 teaspoon of powdered mustard
- 1/3 cup of extra virgin olive oil
- Salt

Steam the cauliflower for about 5 minutes until tender. Once done, rinse it in cold water, then put in ice water to stop from overcooking.

In a 4 inch terrine or mini-loaf pan, put in some cling wrap, leaving enough draping over the edges so you can cover the top later.

Put in 1/4 inch of goat cheese in the bottom of the terrine. Put in some of the cauliflower, then add scoops of more goat cheese, and more cauliflower. Smash everything together and keep repeating until you get to the top. Cover the top with the overhanging cling wrap, then put another terrine and/or some heavy flat weights for 24 hours.

Remove from the terrine pan and slice the goat cheese loaf into 1/4 slices.

To make the vinaigrette, whisk the mustard, balsamic vinegar, salt, and pepper in a bowl. Then, add the olive oil and whisk well. Mix with the greens. Arrange the goat cheese slices beside the greens.

Serves 4.

Roasted Colored Cauliflower [Side Dish]

- 1/2 head of orange cauliflower, cut in 1 inch size pieces
- 1/2 head of purple cauliflower, cut in 1 inch size pieces
- 1/2 head of white cauliflower, cut in 1 inch size pieces
- 1 red onion, chopped
- 1 tablespoon of chopped fresh mint leaves
- 1 clove of garlic, minced
- 5 small Thai hot peppers (or 1/4 teaspoon of cayenne pepper)
- 3 tablespoons of olive oil
- Salt and pepper

Preheat your oven to 450°F.

In a bowl, mix the cauliflower with the olive oil, onion, garlic and peppers.

Add some salt and pepper and put everything in a roasting pan. Roast for about 15 minutes, stirring once or twice until the cauliflower is tender.

Remove from heat and sprinkle with mint.

Serves 4.

www.newfoodcookbook.com

Noodles

Soba
- **Origin and cultivation:** Japanese noodles made with buckwheat
- **Availability:** year-round
- **Appearance:** brown dried noodles, fresh can be found in Japan
- **Flavor:** toothsome noodles with buckwheat flavor
- **Trivia:** other colors exist where the noodle is flavored with green tea, yams or pumpkin

Udon
- **Origin and cultivation:** Japanese noodles made with wheat flour
- **Availability:** year-round, often sold frozen especially in Japanese groceries
- **Appearance:** thick white noodles
- **Flavor:** mild
- **Trivia:** brought to Japan from China over 1,000 years ago

Dang Myun
- **Also known as:** Glass Noodles, Oriental Style Noodle, Korean Vermicelli, Tang Myun, Tangmyun or Sweet Potato Vermicelli
- **Origin and cultivation:** popular in Korea and made out of sweet potato starch
- **Availability:** year-round especially in Korean groceries
- **Appearance:** grayish clear when dry and once cooked
- **Flavor:** flavorless and will absorb whatever they are served with
- **Trivia:** the primary ingredient in the Korean noodle dish Jap Chae

Saifun

- **Also known as:** Cellophane Noodles, Bean Threads, Silver Noodles, Jelly Noodles, Fen Szu, Sohoon or Tanghoon
- **Origin and cultivation:** popular in China and Southeast Asia, made out of mung bean starch
- **Availability:** year-round especially in Asian groceries
- **Appearance:** translucent white when dry, transparent if boiled and Styrofoam if fried
- **Flavor:** flavorless and will absorb whatever they are served with
- **Trivia:** will puff up many times their size when fried

NOODLES

COLD SOBA WITH DIPPING SAUCE [Main Course]

- 1 package of soba noodle (12 ounces)
- 1/2 cup soy sauce
- 4 inch piece of dried kelp
- 1/2 cup of dried bonito flakes (Japanese dried and shaved fish)
- 2 shiitake mushrooms
- 2 tablespoons of mirin (a Japanese sweet rice wine
- 2 scallions, minced
- 1 inch of fresh ginger, minced

First make the dipping sauce, which in Japan is called tsuyu. Bring 4 cups of water to a boil. Add the soy sauce, kelp, and dried bonito flakes.

Remove the root end of the mushrooms and discard. Roughly chop the mushrooms and add to the boiling stock. Simmer for 15 minutes then strain. Discard the kelp, bonito flakes and mushrooms.

To the clear stock, add the mirin and simmer for another couple of minutes to boil off the alcohol, then remove from heat and allow to cool in the refrigerator.

While the dipping sauce is cooling, make the noodles by boiling according to the package's instructions. Cool the noodles by rinsing with cold water.

Put the drained noodles on individual plates. Serve the dipping sauce in 4 individual bowls. Evenly distribute the scallions and ginger amongst the dipping sauce bowls. To eat, use chopsticks to grab a bundle of noodles and dip into the sauce.

Serves 4.

UDON SOUP [Starter]

- 2 packages of frozen udon noodles
- 4 slices of Japanese fish cake (generally found frozen), sliced
- 2 thick slices of roast pork (about 1/3 pound from the deli)
- 2 tablespoons of nori (roasted) seaweed, julienned
- 2 tablespoons of diced scallions
- 4 fresh shiitake mushrooms, stems discarded and sliced
- 3 cups of chicken stock

Once the ingredients are sliced and diced, bring the chicken stock to a boil.

To the broth, add the steamed fish cake slices, noodles and mushrooms and simmer for a minute or two. Then, remove from the heat.

Use tongs to put the noodles in 2 bowls. Top with the fish cake and mushrooms. Pour in the chicken stock and finish by adding the pork, nori and scallions.

Serves 2.

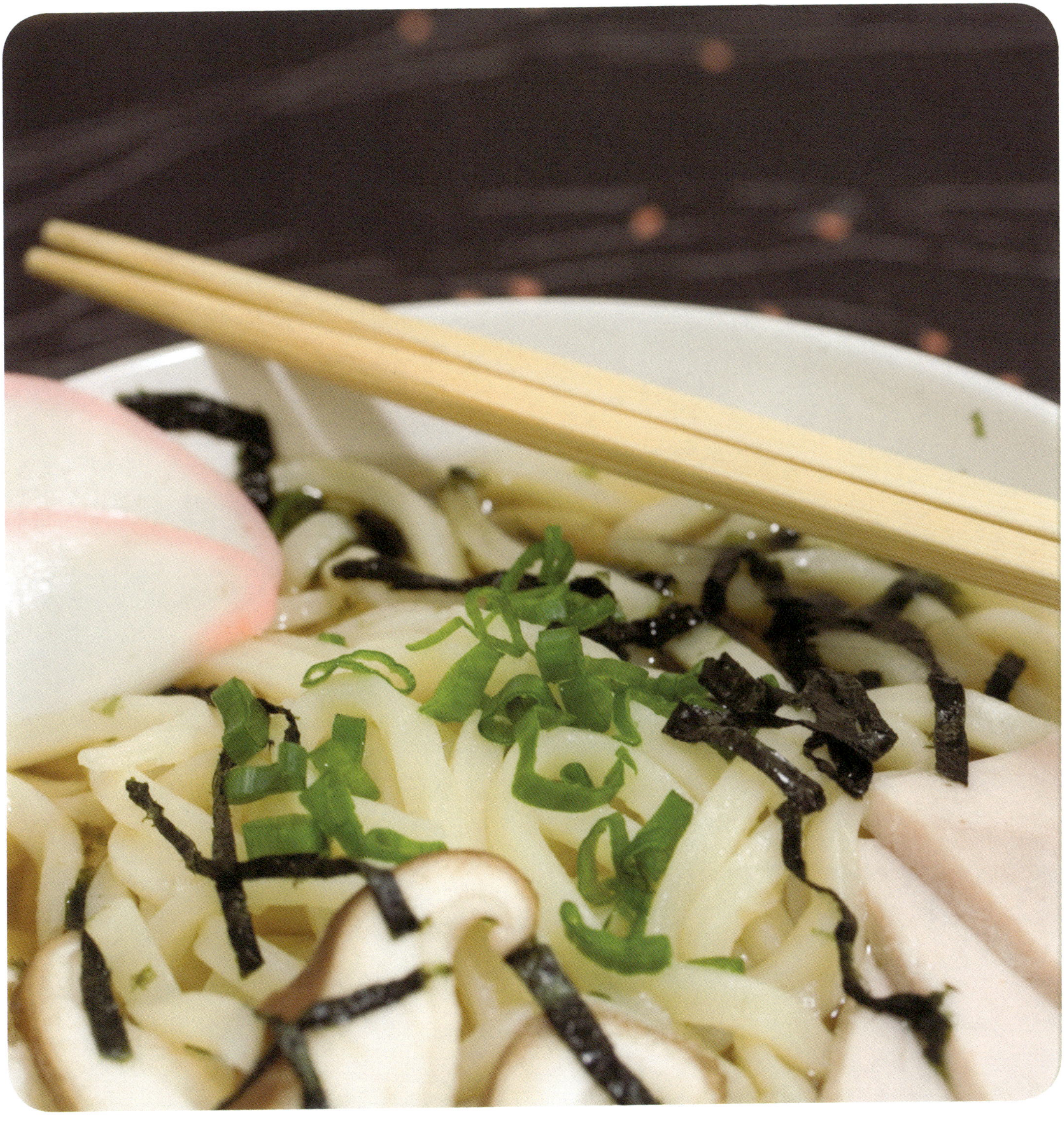

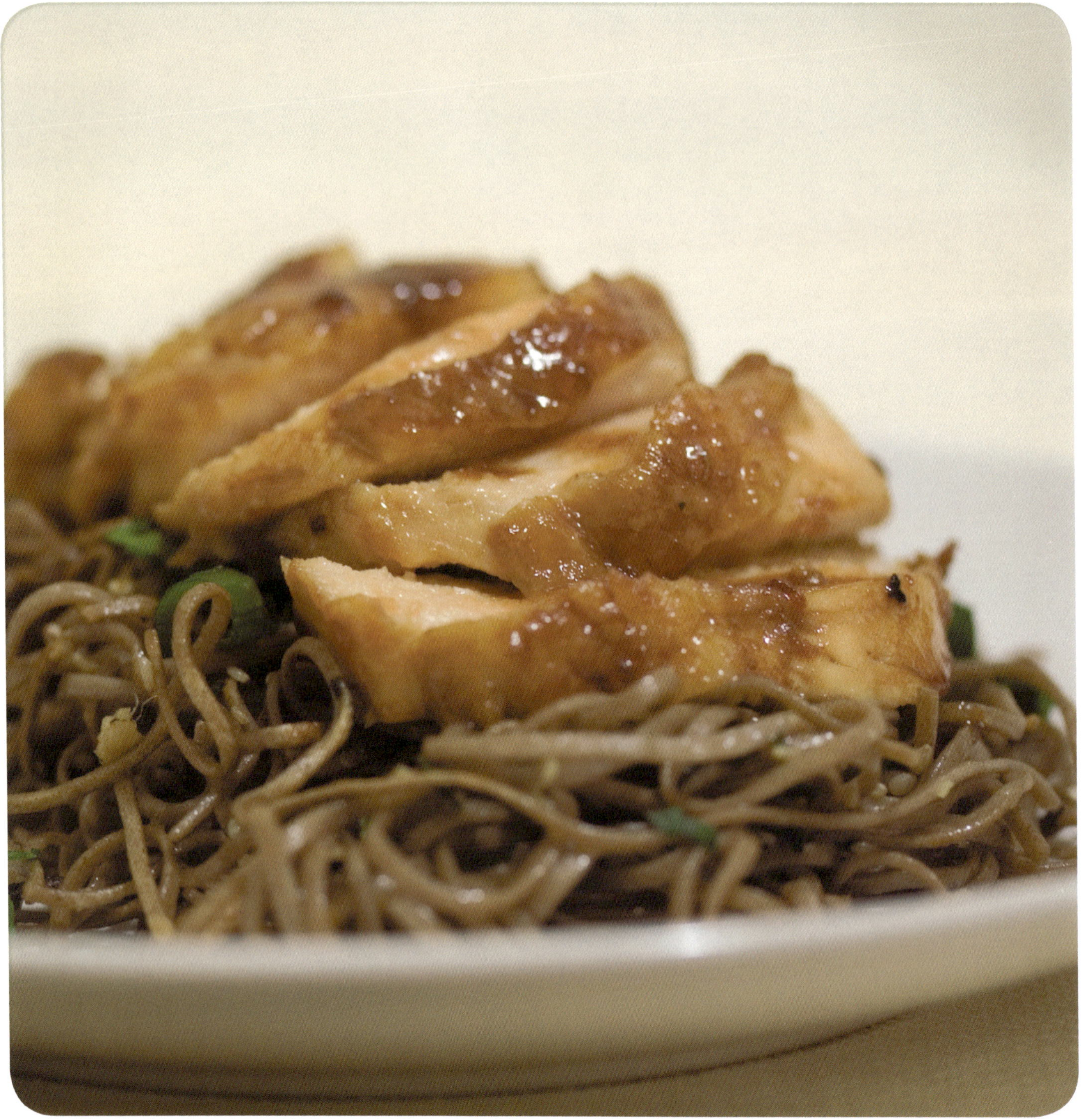

Teriyaki Chicken with Crispy Soba Noodles [Main Course]

- 4 chicken breasts, split
- 1 tablespoon of vegetable oil for cooking the chicken
- 2 tablespoons of sesame oil
- 1/2 package (6 ounces) of soba noodles
- 3 tablespoons of roasted sesame seeds
- 6 scallions, green parts only, chopped
- 4 tablespoons of flat leaf parsley, chopped
- 1 tablespoon of fresh ginger, minced

For the teriyaki sauce:

- 6 tablespoons of soy sauce
- 4 tablespoons of mirin (a Japanese sweet rice wine used for cooking)
- 2 tablespoons of sugar
- 1 tablespoon of fresh ginger, minced

Carefully cut the meat from the bone of the chicken breasts, leaving the skin on. Discard the bones or use them to make stock.

Make the teriyaki sauce by whisking the soy sauce, mirin, sugar, and ginger. Marinate the boneless chicken in the sauce for 20 minutes.

While the chicken is marinating, boil the noodles according to the package directions, probably around 3 minutes. Drain the noodles. Then, in a big non-stick pan on medium-low heat, add 2 tablespoons of sesame oil, sesame seeds, scallions, parsley, ginger, and noodles. Stir occasionally with a pasta spoon or chopsticks for about 15 minutes until they start getting crispy.

While the noodles are getting crispy, make the chicken. Take the chicken out of the teriyaki sauce (but don't throw out the sauce). Add the vegetable oil to a heavy pan and bring up to medium-high heat. Sear the chicken skin side down for 3 minutes until brown. Then flip and sear for 2 minutes. Then, put a lid on the pan and cook covered on very low heat for 8 minutes.

Remove the cover, spoon out some of the grease and add the teriyaki marinade. Simmer for a few more minutes until the sauce is looking like a glaze, and the chicken is cooked through (interior temperature of 165°F).

Serves 4.

NOODLES

SAIFUN STIR FRY [Main Course]

- 1 package of saifun (mung bean threads) noodles, about 6 ounces
- 1 pound of boneless and skinless chicken thighs, cut into 1 inch pieces
- 2 cloves of garlic, minced
- 2 tablespoons of fresh ginger, minced
- 4 baby bok choy, roughly chopped
- 8 shiitake mushrooms, stems discarded and roughly chopped
- 6 scallions, white parts chopped
- 1 cup of snap peas
- 4 carrots, peeled and sliced
- 4 tablespoons of soy sauce
- 4 tablespoons of sesame oil

Make a marinade by combining 2 tablespoons of soy sauce, 1 tablespoon of sesame oil, 1 minced clove of garlic, and 1 tablespoon of ginger. Marinate the chicken for at least 30 minutes if not 2 hours in the refrigerator.

Soak the saifun noodles in hot water for 15 minutes until they are clear, then drain.

Bring some water to boil in a 4 quart pot, you'll use this to boil the noodles later.

In a wok or big heavy pot on high heat, add 2 tablespoons of sesame oil and once hot, add half of the drained pieces of chicken. Cook 3 or 4 minutes until the chicken is done. Remove the chicken to a bowl and keep warm. Repeat with the second half of chicken and also remove.

Add the remaining 1 tablespoon of sesame oil to the same pot and then the vegetables (1 minced clove of garlic, 1 tablespoon of fresh ginger, bok choy, shiitake mushrooms, scallions, snap peas and carrots). Cook on high heat, stirring occasionally for about 5 minutes until the vegetables are done.

While the vegetables are cooking away, add the drained soaked noodles to boiling water in the 4 quart pot and boil for 1 minute until done. Drain.

Then, add the remaining 2 tablespoons of soy sauce and chicken to the vegetables, remove from heat and stir.

Serve the stir fry on top of individual scoops of noodles.

Serves 4.

Fried Saifun Spaghetti Bruschetta [Starter]

- 1/2 package of saifun noodles (about 3 ounces)
- 2 tomatoes
- 1/2 teaspoon of garlic, minced
- 5 basil leaves, julienned
- 1 to 2 cups of vegetable oil
- Salt and pepper

You can deep fry the noodles a few hours in advance if you like, but you should serve immediately after mixing the noodles with the tomato mixture.

Using your hands, tear the noodles into little bundles. Put the vegetable oil in the pan until it is 2 inches deep. Heat on medium-high because you'll want the oil to be at 375°F. Test the oil once it seems hot by putting in a few individual pieces of saifun noodle. If it immediately puffs up in a few seconds, then the oil is hot enough. If not, try again in a minute.

Fry a golf ball sized bit of noodles at a time until they puff up and float to the top, stirring if there are bits that aren't fried. Each batch will only take a few seconds to puff. Remove and put on a paper towel. Repeat until all the noodles are fried.

Peel the tomatoes by dunking in boiling water for about 30 seconds. Then run under cold water and remove the peel. Cut in half and carefully remove the seeds. Dice the tomato.

In a small bowl, mix the tomatoes with the garlic, basil, salt and pepper. Mix the noodles with the tomato mixture and serve immediately.

Serves 4.

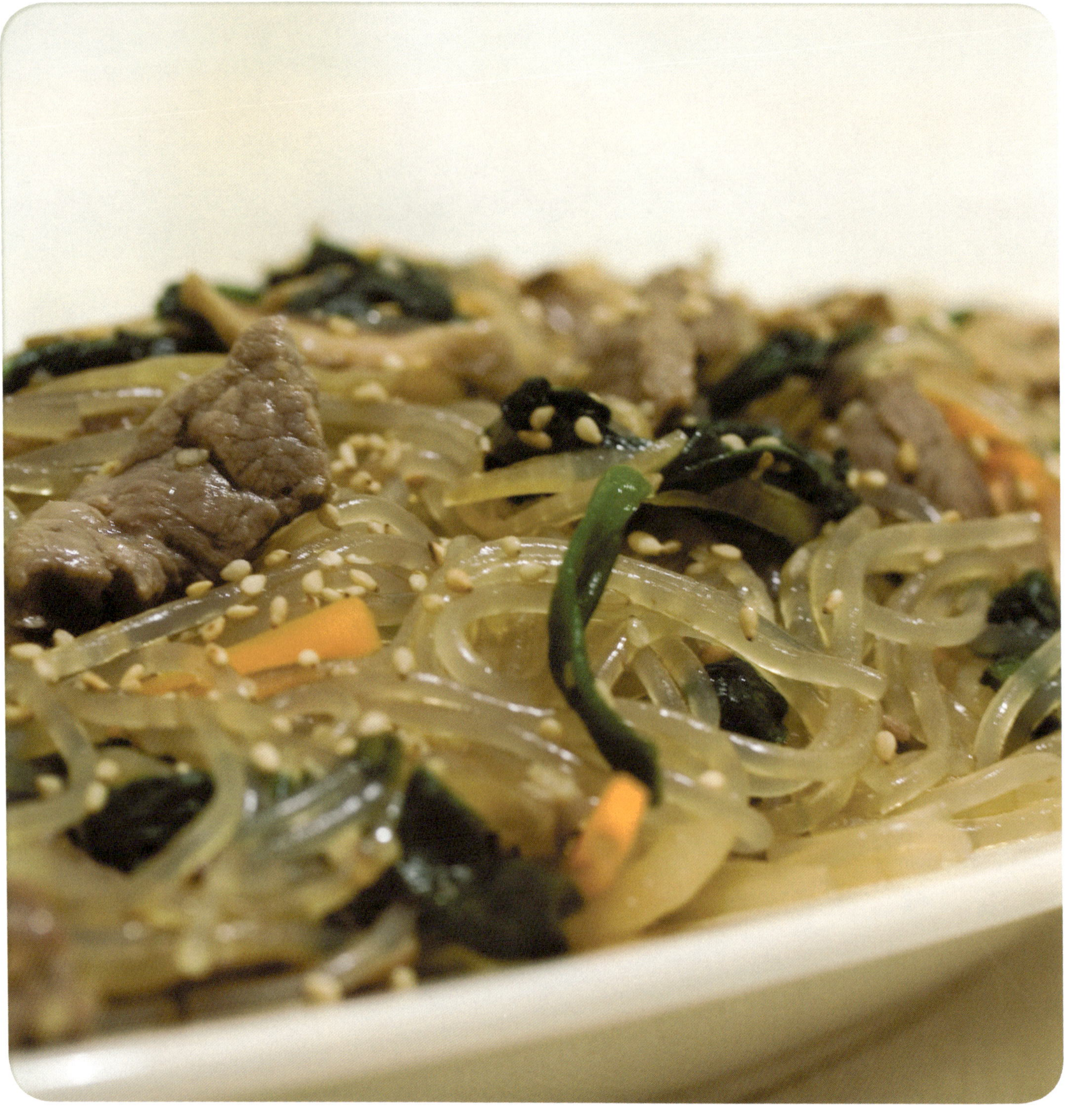

Jap Chae [Main Course]

- 1 pack (12 ounces) Dang Myun
- 1 big onion, sliced
- 3 carrots
- 1 bunch of spinach
- 1/2 pound of beef (sirloin will do nicely), sliced into 1/8 inch thin slices
- 1 bunch of scallions
- 6 fresh shiitake mushrooms, sliced
- 2 tablespoons of sesame oil
- 1 teaspoon of sesame seeds
- 1 tablespoon of soy sauce

For the marinade:
- 3 tablespoons of soy sauce
- 1/2 teaspoon of sugar
- 1 tablespoon of sesame oil
- 1 teaspoon of roasted sesame seeds
- 1 clove of garlic, minced

First, bring some water to a boil, turn off the heat, and put in the noodles to soak for 30 minutes.

Marinate the beef and mushrooms for 20 minutes by whisking together the marinade ingredients and adding the beef and mushrooms.

While the beef is marinating and the noodles soaking, julienne the carrots. Wash the spinach. Cut the green parts of the scallions into 2 inch pieces.

In a big pan, add the 2 tablespoons of sesame oil, put on high heat and once hot, cook the mushrooms and beef for 2 minutes. Then, add the spinach, onion, scallions and carrots. Stir for another minute or two until the vegetables are soft and the beef is cooked through. Turn off the heat.

Drain the noodles and cut them in half with kitchen shears, then add them to the pan. Mix with the vegetables while adding 1 teaspoon of sesame seeds and 1 tablespoon of soy sauce. Put on a nice serving platter.

Serves 4.

Greens

Shiso
- **Also known as:** Perilla, Purple Mint, Beefsteak Plant, Chinese Basil, Deulkkae, Wild Coleus or Silam
- **Origin and cultivation:** herb in the mint family especially popular in Asia
- **Availability:** year-round, especially in Japanese groceries
- **Appearance:** green spiky leaf, can also be purple
- **Flavor:** distinctive unique sweet mint like flavor with hints of fennel
- **Trivia:** green plastic leaf dividers commonly used on sushi platters in the U.S. are actually a replacement for genuine shiso

SPROUTS
- **Origin and cultivation:** harvested when they are between 4 and 5 days old. New varieties of seeds and beans are being introduced as commercial sprouts constantly
- **Availability:** year-round
- **Appearance:** little mini plants
- **Flavor:** often resembles the adult seed or bean
- **Trivia:** eaten for over thousands of years

Shoots
- **Origin and cultivation:** harvested around 14 days old, often from sweet peas or snow peas
- **Availability:** spring at farmers markets
- **Appearance:** tiny plants
- **Flavor:** fresh flavor resembling the adult seed or bean
- **Trivia:** very popular in China

MICROGREENS
- **Origin and cultivation:** 14 and 20 days old, as opposed to baby greens like mesclun mix which are harvested after 35 days. Microgreens exist for all of the same greens that are in mesclun mixes
- **Availability:** year-round
- **Appearance:** tiny lettuce leaves
- **Flavor:** resembling the older salad greens, but often more intense, sometimes spicy
- **Trivia:** you can buy kits to grow microgreens at home

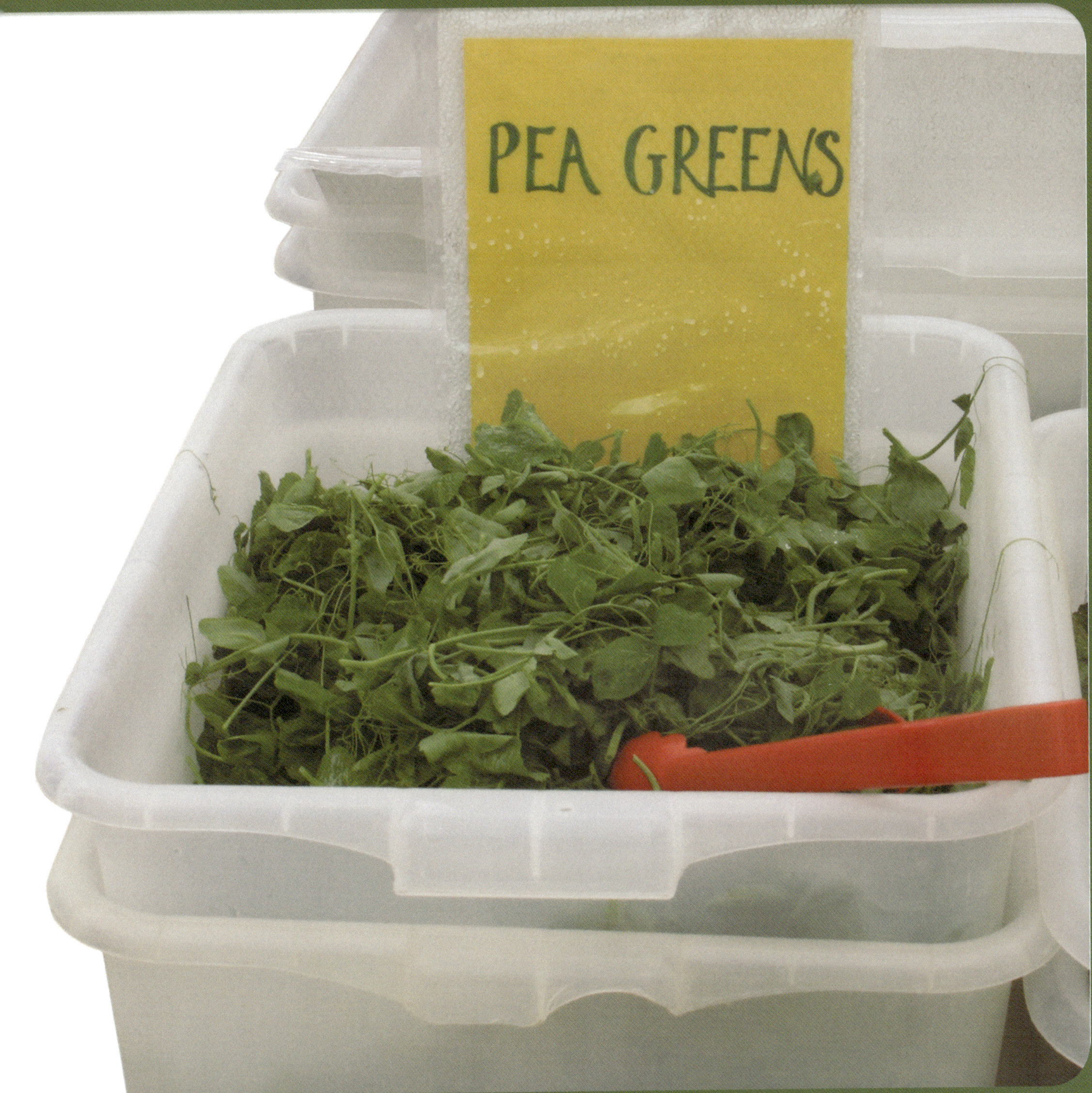
PEA GREENS

GREENS

MICROGREENS IN TINY PARMESAN BOWLS [Starter]

- 1 cup of microgreens
- 1 cup of freshly grated Parmesan Reggiano
- 4 round small glass ramekins
- 4 teaspoons of cider vinegar
- 1 teaspoon of powdered mustard
- 1/3 cup of extra virgin olive oil
- Salt and pepper

Preheat the oven to 350°F.

Make each Parmesan bowl individually. Use a Teflon pan on medium heat. Add 1/4 cup of grated cheese in a 5 inch diameter disk in the middle and wait until it melts. Gently loosen with a spatula and drape over a glass ramekin. Let cool for 10 minutes.

Repeat the process to make 4 more bowls.

To make the vinaigrette, whisk the mustard, cider vinegar, olive oil, salt and pepper.

Toss the vinaigrette with the microgreens and put some into each Parmesan bowl.

Serves 4.

MICROGREENS ON FRIED GOAT CHEESE MEDALLIONS [Starter]

- 1 cup of microgreens
- 4 ounce goat cheese log, cold
- 1 egg, beaten
- 1 cup of breadcrumbs with salt and pepper added
- 4 teaspoons of aged balsamic vinegar
- 1 teaspoon of powdered mustard
- 1/3 cup of hazelnut oil
- 3 tablespoons of olive oil for frying goat cheese
- Salt and pepper

To make the goat cheese medallions, carefully cut the goat cheese log into 1/4 slices. If you have crumbly cheese, then put the slices in your palms and form them into medallions. Dip the slices into the egg, then into the breadcrumbs. Do this to all the slices and keep them in a few stacks off to the side.

Using a small heavy pan, pour enough olive oil so that there is about an 1/8 inch. Heat on medium-high. When the oil is good and hot put in four of the medallions. Fry on one side for 20 seconds, gently flip with tongs, and fry another 15 seconds so that both sides are light brown. Then, remove and dry on paper towels. Repeat with the next batch. Don't fry too long or the cheese will melt out.

Make the vinaigrette. In a bowl, whisk the mustard, balsamic vinegar, hazelnut oil, salt, and pepper. Toss the microgreens with the vinaigrette. Then, assemble the fried goat cheese on a plate and put the greens on top.

Serves 2.

Cucumber Salad with Feta and Shiso [Starter]

- 8 ounces of feta cheese in 1/4 inch cubes
- 5 shiso leaves
- 2 cucumbers peeled, seeded and cut in 1/4 inch cubes
- 1/4 cup of red onion, sliced extremely thin
- 1/4 cup of extra virgin olive oil
- 1 tablespoon of rice vinegar
- Salt and pepper

In a bowl, mix the feta, cucumbers, chopped shiso, and onion. Put 2 of the whole shiso leaves on 2 plates and put the salad mixture on top.

Make a vinaigrette out of the vinegar, olive oil salt and pepper. Whisk and pour over the salad at the last possible moment before eating.

Serves 2.

First, take the sliced onion and soak in ice water because this takes off some of the edge. Soak for 20 minutes then drain well.

Take 3 of the shiso leaves and chop finely. Reserve the other 2 whole leaves.

GREENS

Sautéed Pea Shoots with Baby Carrots and Spring Garlic [Side Dish]

- 3 cups of pea shoots
- 1 bunch of baby carrots
- 2 stalks of spring garlic (or substitute the white part of 3 green onions)
- 2 tablespoons of olive oil
- Salt and pepper

You don't need to peel baby carrots, but cut the greens off leaving a quarter inch of the stalk. Scrub gently with a vegetable brush under running water to scrape off any stringy things and dirt.

To prepare the spring garlic, cut off the bulb and the stem where it starts to turn green. All you'll want to use is the white part of the stem which will probably be about 2 inches. Discard the outermost layer of the white part of the stem. The bulb and the green parts won't be needed. Cut the white part of the stem into thin slices.

In a pan on high heat, put in the olive oil and heat up. Toss in the sliced spring garlic stem, and baby carrots. Sauté for 3 minutes. Then add the pea shoots and sauté for no more than 30 seconds, and finally season with salt and pepper.

Serves 2.

Fruit Macerated with Shiso and Sweet Wine [Dessert]

- 4 shiso leaves, minced
- 2 peaches
- 2 apples
- 2 pears
- 1 cantaloupe melon
- 1 cup of cherries, pitted
- Juice of 1/2 a lemon
- 1 1/2 cup of dessert wine (such as a Sautérnes, Trockenbeerenauslese, Tokaji aszu, or Recioto)

Add the lemon juice and shiso to the wine and mix. Put the wine mixture into a big fruit bowl.

Cut the fruit off the peaches into 1 inch cubes and toss in the fruit bowl. Core the apples and pears, chop into 1 inch cubes and also toss into the wine mixture. Remove the seeds and skin from the cantaloupe and cut into 1 inch pieces. Finally, add the pitted cherries.

Refrigerate for at least 2 hours along with the bottle of leftover wine. If you didn't drink the leftover wine yourself, then you are encouraged to serve it with the macerated fruit.

Serves 8.

Snow Pea Sprout and Radish Salad [Starter]

- 1 cup of snow pea sprouts
- 1 bunch of radishes
- 2 tablespoons of chardonnay white wine vinegar
- 1/3 cup of grape seed oil
- 1 teaspoon of powdered mustard
- Salt and pepper

First, steam the radishes for about 3 minutes then dunk in an ice bath.

Make a vinaigrette by whisking the vinegar, grape seed oil, mustard, salt and pepper.

Mix the snow pea sprouts with the radishes and toss together with the vinaigrette.

Serves 2.

GREENS

Root Vegetables

Colored carrots
- **Origin and cultivation:** the original carrot was probably purple and was cultivated over 5,000 years ago
- **Availability:** summer at farmers markets and some supermarkets
- **Appearance:** white carrots lack pigment; purple (also called maroon) carrots get their color from anthocyanin pigments; yellow carrots get their color from xanthophylls, a carotenoid; red carrots get their color from lycopene, a carotenoid, along with the same pigments in orange carrots which are beta-carotene and alpha carotene
- **Flavor:** like carrots, the colors contribute little flavor
- **Trivia:** Romans used white and purple carrots. By the 14th century in Europe, a variety of colored carrots were being grown including purple, red, yellow, and white, but not orange. Orange carrots didn't exist until the 16th century, where patriotic Dutch farmers bred them in honor of the royal House of Orange. Since the 1990s, because of the hype surrounding antioxidant properties of anthocyanins in purple carrots, they are being grown on a more industrial scale

Blue potatoes
- **Also known as:** Purple Potatoes or Peruvian Purple Potatoes
- **Origin and cultivation:** originally cultivated by ancient Andean Indian civilizations; introduced in North America in the 1970s
- **Appearance:** blue color is from anthocyanin pigments
- **Flavor:** like potatoes, blue color contributes little flavor
- **Trivia:** blue sweet potatoes also exist, often called Okinawa sweet potatoes

Celeriac
- **Also known as:** Celery Root or Knob Celery
- **Origin and cultivation:** a special variety of celery that is grown for the root rather than the stalks, has been cultivated in Europe for hundreds of years
- **Availability:** year-round
- **Appearance:** big ugly knobby root that is a little bigger than a softball, with a dirty brown colored skin
- **Flavor:** has a nice celery and parsley flavor and can be eaten raw or cooked
- **Trivia:** unpopular only because it is ugly before it is peeled

Golden Beets

- **Also known as:** Yellow Beets or Yellow Beetroot
- **Origin and cultivation:** cultivated for centuries in Europe
- **Availability:** year-round
- **Appearance:** like a beet, only yellow, the color is from betaxanthin pigment
- **Flavor:** sweeter flavor than red beets
- **Trivia:** in Europe, a variety of yellow beets were used as animal fodder which led to prejudice that yellow beets were for animals while red were for people

ROOT VEGETABLES

Colored Carrot "Fettuccini" with Tarragon Pesto [Starter]

- 4 white carrots
- 4 yellow carrots
- 4 red carrots
- 4 purple carrots
- 1 clove of garlic
- 1/2 cup of firmly packed tarragon leaves
- 1/4 cup of extra virgin olive oil
- 1 teaspoon of pine nuts
- 3 tablespoons of shredded parmesan
- 1 teaspoon of white vinegar
- Salt and pepper

Peel the carrots. Cut in half or quarters longitudinally so that the fattest side is about the thickness of a nice fettuccini noodle. Then, use a vegetable peeler to slice the carrots into ribbons. Keep each color of carrot separate because you'll cook them separately to avoid the colors bleeding together.

Make the pesto using a food processor or blender. First add the garlic clove and chop up. Then, add the tarragon leaves, pine nuts, parmesan, white vinegar and a dash of salt and pepper. Add about half the olive oil and pulse until blended. Continue adding olive oil until mixed thoroughly.

In a small pot bring a couple of inches of salted water to a simmer. Add the white carrot ribbons and simmer for 2 or 3 minutes until al dente. Remove with tongs, then add the yellow carrots. Then, cook the red carrots and finish with the purple carrots.

Arrange the carrot fettuccini on a plate and drizzle with the tarragon pesto.

Serves 4 as a side dish, warm or cold.

White Carrot Ginger Soup with Chervil and Crispy Prosciutto [Starter]

- 2 bunches of white carrots (about 12 medium sized carrots)
- 1 clove of garlic, minced
- 2 teaspoons minced fresh ginger
- 4 cups of chicken or vegetable stock
- 1 slice of Prosciutto di Parma, juilliened
- 1 tablespoon of olive oil
- 2 tablespoons of fresh chervil
- Salt

Peel the carrots and chop them into 1 inch pieces. Put the stock in a pot and bring to a boil. Add the carrots, garlic, ginger and a little salt and simmer for about 20 minutes until tender.

Use a hand blender, or regular blender and purée the soup until smooth. Taste and add more salt if necessary.

In a small pan, heat the olive oil on medium-high until nice and hot. Add julienned prosciutto slices and fry for a minute until they are crispy.

Put the soup in small bowls and garnish with the prosciutto and chervil.

Serves 4.

Golden Borscht with Goji Berries and Sour Cream [Starter]

- 8 golden beets (about 1 pound)
- 1 small onion, chopped
- 3 carrots, chopped
- 7 cups of water
- Juice of 1 lemon
- Zest of 1 lemon, minced
- 4 tablespoons of sour cream
- 3 tablespoons of goji berries
- Salt and pepper

Peel the beets and use a food processor to shred them.

Put the beets and water in a pot, bring to a boil and simmer for 20 minutes. Add the carrots, lemon zest and onion and simmer for 20 more minutes. Skim off any foam. Remove from heat and add lemon juice, salt and pepper.

You could serve the soup hot, or cold by chilling for a few hours or overnight in the fridge.

When serving, put a tablespoon of sour cream into each bowl and sprinkle with goji berries.

Serves 4.

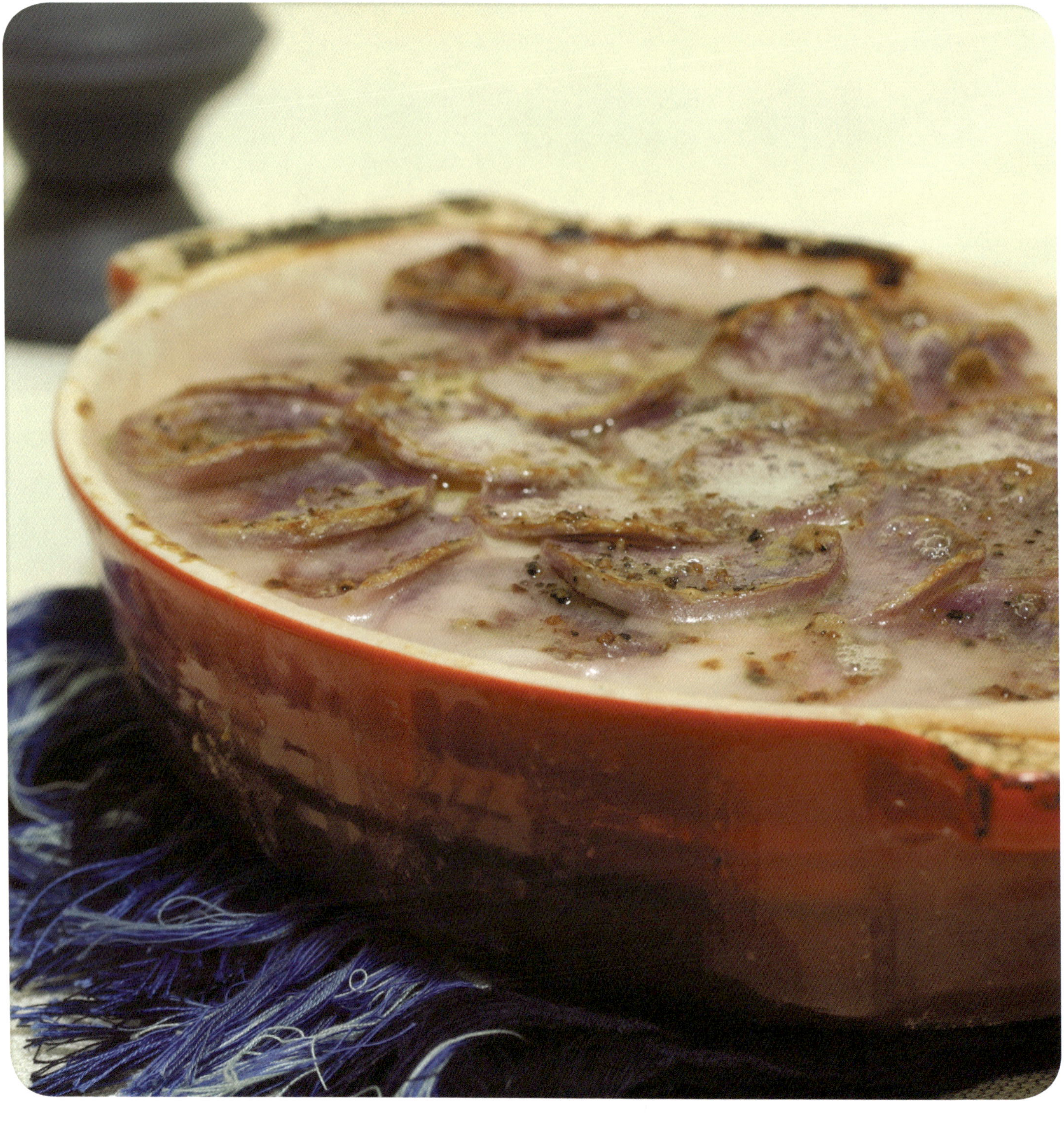

SCALLOPED BLUE POTATOES WITH BLUE CHEESE [Side Dish]

- 1 pound blue potatoes
- 2 tablespoons of flour + a little extra for dusting the casserole
- 4 tablespoons of butter + a little extra to coat the casserole
- 1/4 teaspoon of freshly grated nutmeg
- 1 1/2 cup of milk
- 1/4 cup of crumbled blue cheese
- 1/4 cup of grated white cheddar cheese
- Salt and pepper

Preheat the oven to 375°F.

Coat the inside of the casserole with butter and lightly dust with flour.

In a small saucepan on medium heat, melt 2 tablespoons of the butter and once foaming, add the flour and whisk until there are no lumps. Add a little of the milk, whisking all the while to keep lumps from forming. Then, slowly add the rest of the milk, continuing to stir. Bring to a simmer and continue simmering for about five minutes while stirring fairly regularly.

While the milk is simmering, peel and thinly slice the blue potatoes.

Once the milk has simmered for about 5 minutes and thickened, fold in the cheese a spoonful or two at a time. Once fully incorporated, turn off the heat, then mix in the nutmeg, salt and pepper.

Put a layer or two of potatoes on the bottom of a 9 inch oval casserole. Pour on a bit of the cheese sauce, and then add another layer of potatoes. Repeat with alternating layers of cheese sauce and potatoes until the casserole is filled. On the top layer of potatoes, dot with the remaining 2 tablespoons of butter. Cover with aluminum foil.

Bake for 45 minutes until tender.

Remove the foil and put under the broiler for 5 minutes until golden brown.

Serves 4 to 6.

ROOT VEGETABLES

ROOT VEGETABLES

Celeriac Soup with Leeks and Bacon [Starter]

- 1 big celeriac (2 pounds)
- 3 leeks
- 2 cloves of garlic, minced
- 1 tablespoon of butter
- 3 pieces of cooked bacon, chopped
- 1 quart of chicken stock
- 3 tablespoons of crème fraîche
- Salt and pepper

Chop the tough outer green leaves and bottom bulb from the leeks and discard. Clean the leeks well and chop.

Peel the celeriac and cut into 1 inch cubes.

In a medium sized pot, heat the butter on medium-low and add the leeks and garlic and cook for 5 minutes. Then, add the celeriac, stock, salt and pepper. Bring to a boil, then put heat on low, cover, and simmer for about 25 to 30 minutes until the celeriac is tender.

Remove from heat. Add the crème fraîche, then use a hand blender to purée.

Garnish each bowl with bacon.

Serves 4.

Purple Carrot Cake alla Romanesca [Dessert]

For the carrot cake:
- 1 1/2 cup of shredded purple carrots
- 2 1/2 cups of flour
- 1 1/4 cup of sugar
- 1 teaspoon of baking powder
- 1 teaspoon of baking soda
- 4 eggs
- 1 teaspoon of freshly ground cinnamon
- 1/4 teaspoon of ground dry ginger
- 1 teaspoon of grated nutmeg
- 1 cup of raisins
- 1 cup of pine nuts
- 1 cup of vegetable oil
- Dash of salt
- 1 tablespoon of butter
- 1 tablespoon of flour to dust the pan

For the icing:
- 4 tablespoons of butter, room temperature
- 8 ounces of mascarpone cheese
- 1 cup of powdered sugar

Toast the pine nuts in a toaster or a small pan for a minute or two until the aroma is enhanced.

Preheat the oven to 350°F.

Use the tablespoon of butter to coat the inside of a 9X9 cake pan, then dust with flour.

Take the shredded carrots and put in a microwave safe bowl. Add a tablespoon of water, cover and microwave for 1 minute to steam them and extract some of the color. Let cool.

Use an electric mixer with a whisk attachment to mix together the flour, baking powder, baking soda, cinnamon, ginger, nutmeg and a dash of salt.

In another, and bigger, mixing bowl, use the electric mixer whisk to mix the sugar and eggs for 20 seconds. Next, while still running the electric mixer at a reasonably high speed, drizzle in the vegetable oil, very slowly at first. You are creating an emulsion so take your time to make sure the oil combines with the egg and sugar mixture before you speed up adding more oil.

Once the oil is incorporated, add the flour, carrots, raisins and pine nuts to the bowl. Using a rubber spatula, stir everything by hand until combined.

Pour the cake batter into the cake pan and bake for 40 minutes or until a toothpick in the center comes out clean.

Put the cake pan on a wire rack and cool for a couple of hours before starting on the icing.

Make the icing by using an electric mixer to whip the butter, mascarpone and powdered sugar together until it lightens up and starts looking like icing, probably after about 1 minute.

Put the icing on the cooled cake.

Serves 8.

Heritage Meats & Farm Raised Game

Berkshire pork
- **Also known as:** Kurobuta (in Japan)
- **Origin and cultivation:** named after Berkshire, in England, where it was raised over 300 years ago
- **Availability:** year-round
- **Appearance:** marbled pork
- **Flavor:** richer than typical pork
- **Trivia:** Oliver Cromwell's favorite pork

Goat meat
- **Also known as:** Chevon
- **Origin and cultivation:** domesticated over 10,000 years ago, often comes from specific breeds such as Boers, Kikos and Tennessee Fainting Goats, which are different than breeds used for their milk
- **Availability:** year-round
- **Appearance:** red meat
- **Flavor:** similar to mild lamb
- **Trivia:** fastest growing type of meat in the U.S. and possibly in the world

Silkie Chickens
- **Also known as:** Black Boned Chicken
- **Origin and cultivation:** perhaps originally bred in Asia
- **Availability:** year-round in Chinatowns
- **Appearance:** dark blue-black skin, black bones and dark meat, the skin turns black when cooked
- **Flavor:** like chicken
- **Trivia:** have 5 toes, most chickens only have 4 toes

Squab
- **Also known as:** Rock Pigeon
- **Origin and cultivation:** young pigeons, usually harvested when they are around 4 weeks old
- **Availability:** year-round
- **Appearance:** smaller than a Cornish game hen, bigger than a quail
- **Flavor:** have a juicy, rich and mildly gamy flavor
- **Trivia:** the first domesticated poultry, predating chickens

Pheasants
- **Origin and cultivation:** originally wild in Asia, are now being farm raised
- **Availability:** year-round
- **Appearance:** depending on their age can be the size of a Cornish game hen, or larger
- **Flavor:** have a pleasant, mildly gamy flavor
- **Trivia:** are not native to Europe or the Americas, where they were introduced into the wild as game birds

Ibérico de Bellota
- **Origin and cultivation:** black-footed pigs from Spain; lomo is the meat from the pig's loins while Jamon is the ham
- **Availability:** now available for export to the U.S. because of a new U.S. federally approved processing facility in Spain
- **Appearance:** looks like prosciutto
- **Flavor:** wonderful rich nutty flavor and the hams are considered one of the finest in the world
- **Trivia:** the pigs are free-range, wandering around oak mountain meadows eating acorns which impart the superior flavor

HERITAGE MEATS & FARM RAISED GAME

LOMO OLIVE BITES [Starter]

- 1/2 pound of thinly sliced Ibérico de Bellota Lomo
- 4 cups of pitted olives
- 2 tablespoons of your favorite mustard
- Toothpicks

Dab each Lomo slice with a touch of mustard and wrap around an olive. Hold together with a toothpick.

Serves 8.

SILKIE BLUE-BLACK CHICKEN WITH SILKY GARLIC [Main Course]

- 2 Silkie chickens, halved
- 52 cloves of garlic (13 per person), separated from the head and unpeeled
- 1 bouquet garni (a bay leaf, sprig of fresh thyme and sprig of rosemary tied together)
- 4 tablespoons of olive oil
- 1 large onion, chopped
- 2/3 cup of dry white wine
- A baguette
- Salt and pepper

Marinate the chicken in a mix of the white wine, garlic cloves, bouquet garni, olive oil, salt and pepper for 1 or 2 hours in the refrigerator.

Preheat the oven to 350°F.

Add the chopped onion to the bottom of a Dutch oven, or other heavy casserole with a lid. Add the chicken, and then pour in the marinade including the bouquet garni and garlic cloves.

Cover and roast for 1 hour and 30 minutes. Discard the bouquet garni before serving.

Serve with toasted slices of baguette for spreading on the roasted garlic which will have a smooth silky texture.

Serves 4.

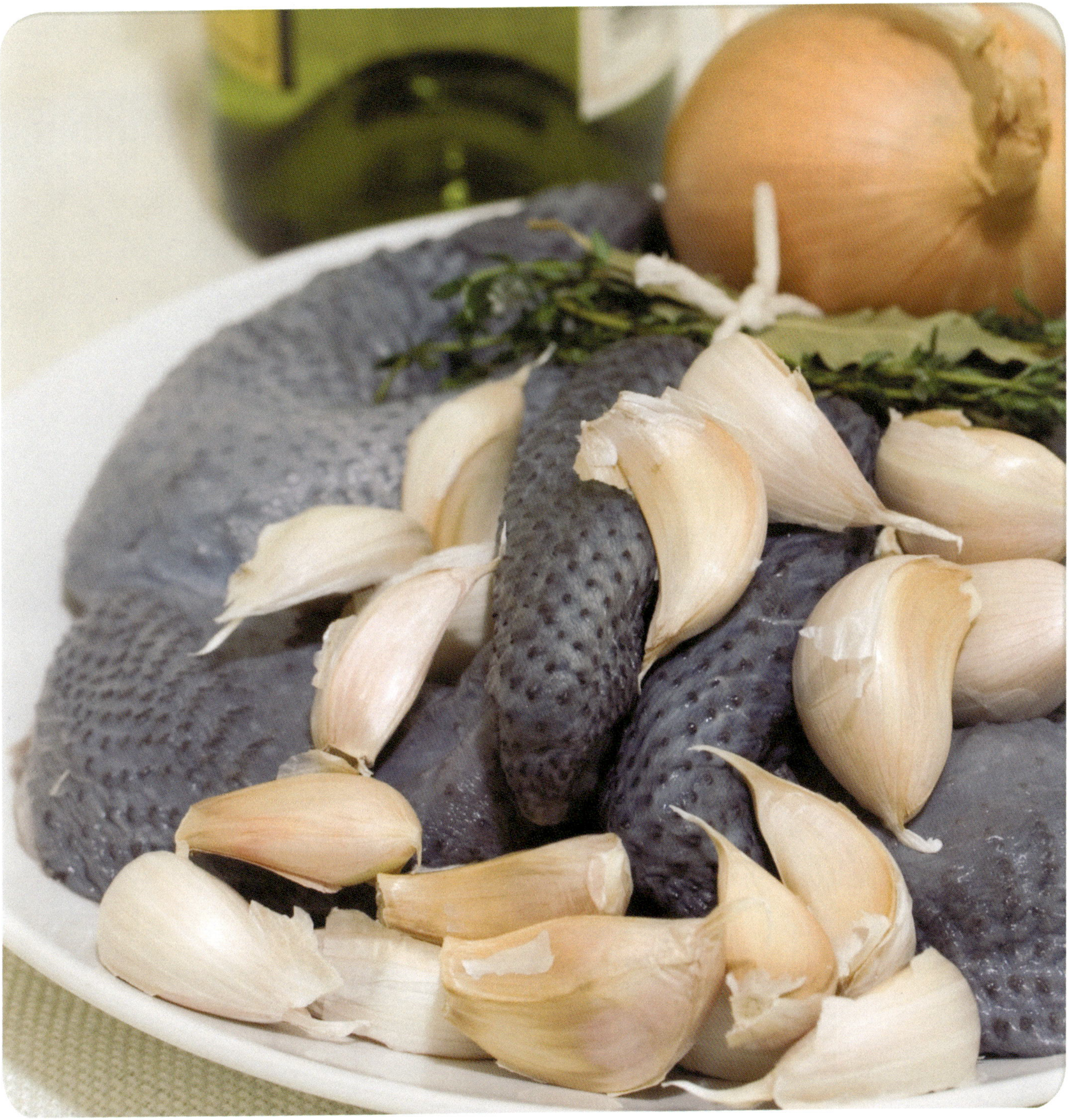

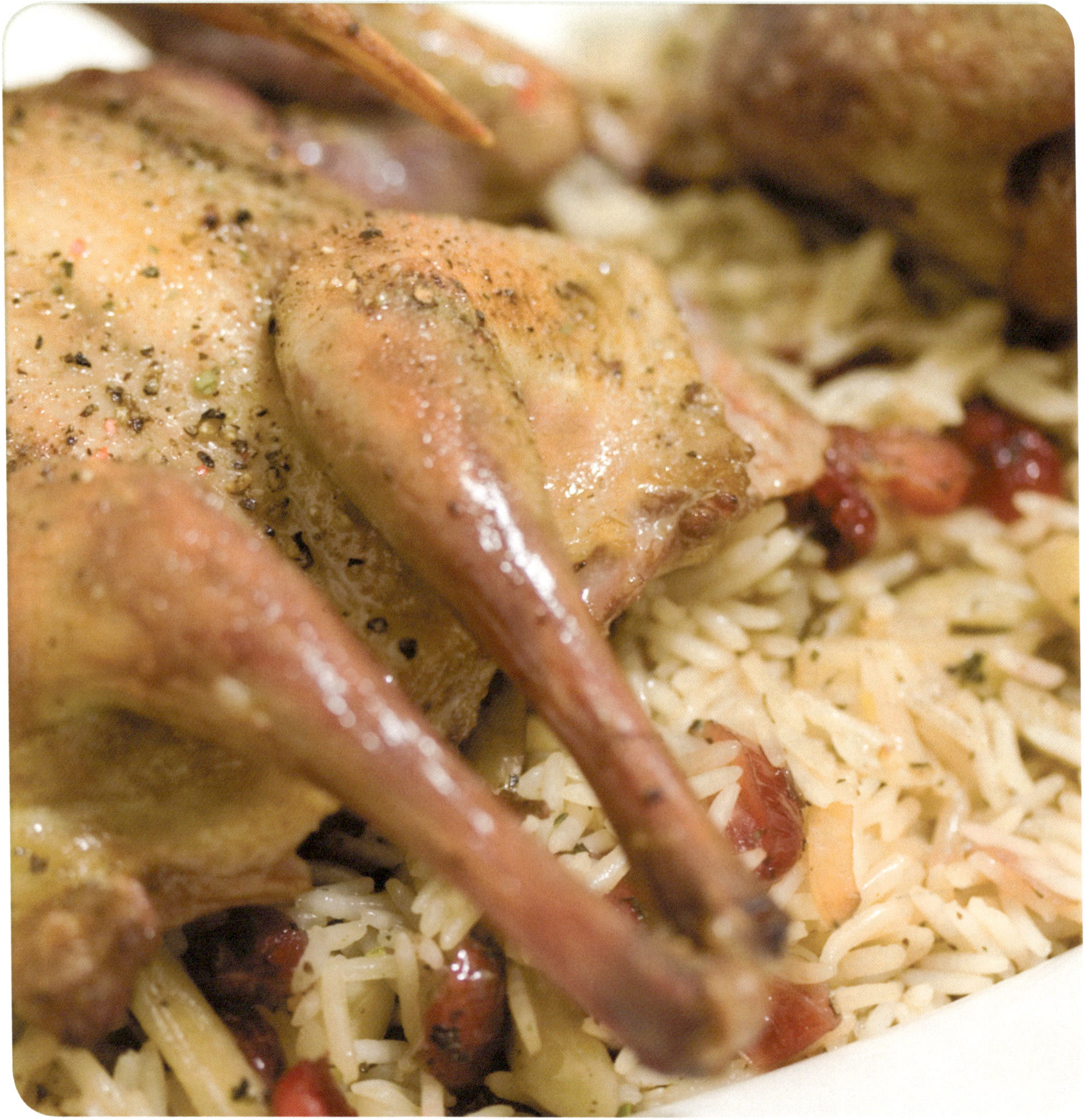

Squab Pilaf [Main Course]

- 2 squab
- 2 tablespoons of olive oil
- 1 shallot, minced
- 1 cup of basmati rice
- 1 teaspoon of Provençal herbs (herb mix including thyme, tarragon, lavender, and/or rosemary)
- 1/4 cup of slivered almonds
- 3 tablespoons of dried cranberries
- 1/4 cup of bourbon
- 1 1/2 cup of chicken stock
- Salt and pepper

Rinse the rice until the water runs clear and soak in water until you need it, which is going to be in about 10 minutes.

Split the squab on their back with poultry shears, then flatten. Remove the rib bones if you are skilled. Season both sides with salt and pepper.

Put a big pot on a medium high burner and heat up the oil. Then, add one squab skin side down and sear for a few minutes until turning brown, flip and brown the other side too. Remove and put in a small roasting pan and repeat the searing process with the second bird. Don't clean the pot because you're going to use it the way it is in a few minutes.

Finish roasting the squab on a baking sheet in a 325°F oven until the internal temperature is 165°F (probably after around 25 minutes).

While the squab is roasting, in the same pot that you seared the squab, and on medium, sauté the shallot until soft, add the almonds and cook for 30 seconds until they are brown. Pour in the bourbon and reduce by half while stirring up the brown bits stuck to the bottom of the pan. Add the chicken stock, herbs, salt and pepper and bring to a boil. Then, put the heat on as low as possible and add the drained rice, along with the cranberries. Cover tightly and cook for about 15 minutes.

Once the rice is done, lightly fluff. Serve the squab on top of the rice.

Serves 2.

ROASTED HERITAGE BERKSHIRE PORK CHOPS WITH APPLE PAN SAUCE [Main Course]

- 2 Berkshire pork chops, 1 inch thick
- 1 apple
- 1/4 cup Calvados
- 1/2 cup of demi-glace
- 1 teaspoon of sage, chopped
- 2 tablespoons of butter
- 1 tablespoon of olive oil
- Salt and pepper

Preheat the oven to 350°F.

Pat the pork chops dry and sprinkle with salt and pepper.

In an ovenproof pan, put in 1 tablespoon of butter and olive oil, and on high heat, sear the pork chops for 2 minutes on each side, until nice and brown.

Spoon out most of the fat in the pan and put the pan in the oven. Roast the pork chops for 10 minutes, until the internal temperature is 140°F. Berkshire pork is best at this temperature, which is lower than the USDA recommended temperature of 160°F. If you are a concerned person, then you are better off sticking with 160°F.

A couple minutes before you think the pork chops are done, you can peel, core and chop the apple into little pieces.

Take the pan out of the oven, remove the pork chops and keep warm.

In the now empty pan used to roast the pork, put back on a burner on medium-high heat, and then add the apples, sage and remaining tablespoon of butter. Caramelize for a minute or two. Then, add the Calvados and reduce by half to burn off the alcohol. Add the demi-glace, any juices in the bowl from the reserved pork, and salt and pepper. Reduce for minute or two until it is nice and thick.

Spoon the sauce over the pork chops and serve.

Serves 2.

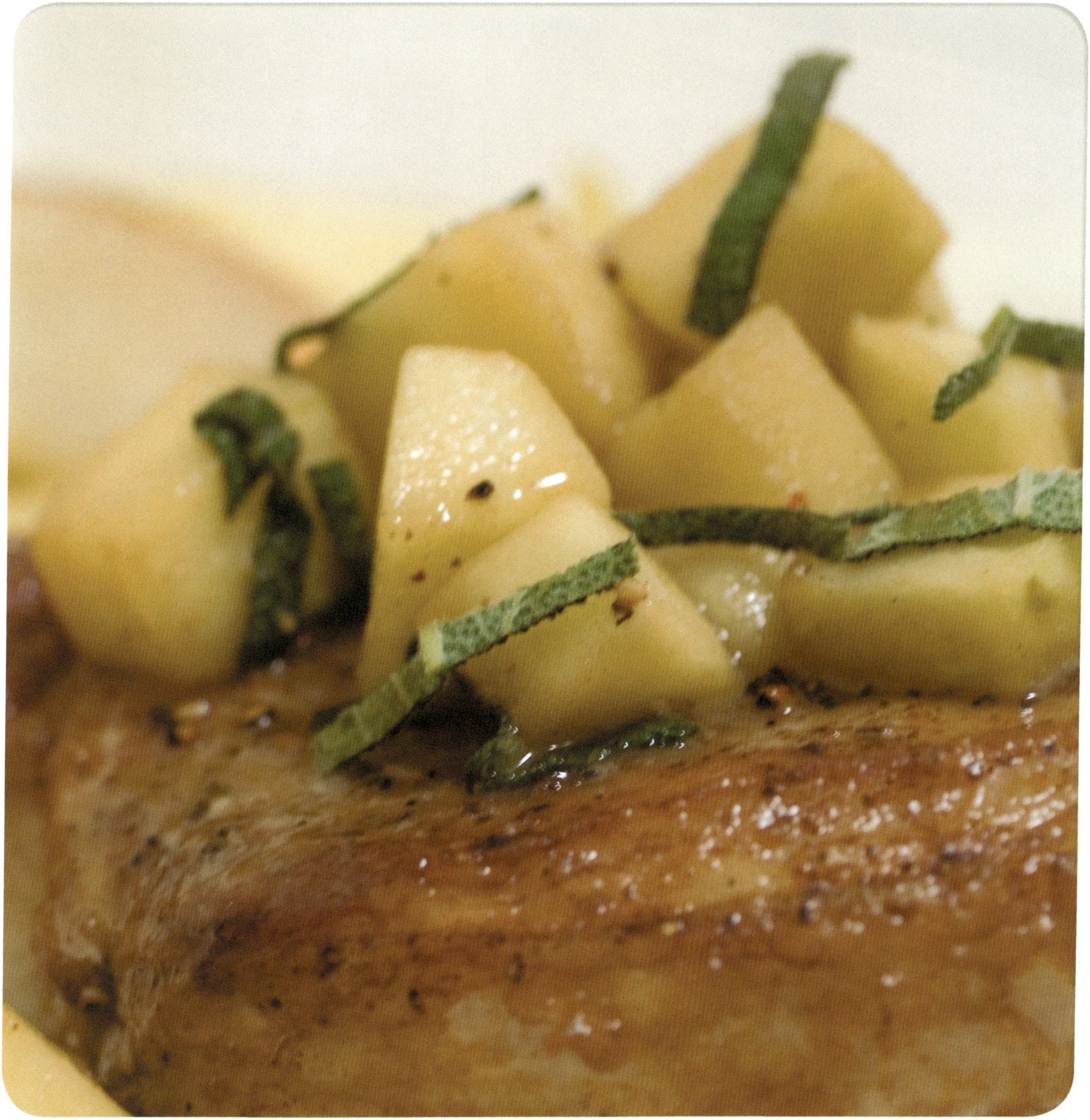

HERITAGE MEATS & FARM RAISED GAME

IBÉRICO DE BELLOTA WITH FETTUCINNI [Main Course]

- 1 pound of fresh fettuccini
- 1/2 pound of Jamon Ibérico de Bellota, sliced thin
- 3 tablespoons of butter
- 2 cups of grated Parmesan Reggiano cheese
- 1 cup of tightly packed spinach
- Salt and pepper

Wash and dry the spinach.

Slice the Ibérico de Bellota into little strips.

Cook the pasta. When done, drain. While the empty pasta pot is still hot, add the butter and spinach then put the drained hot pasta back into the pot. Add the cheese, Ibérico de Bellota, salt and pepper. Mix well.

The hot pasta will steam the spinach and melt the cheese and butter. Serve immediately.

Serves 4.

NEW FOOD – CONTEMPORARY RECIPES, FASHIONABLE INGREDIENTS

Roast Pheasant with Cumberland Sauce [Main Course]

For the pheasant:
- One 3.5 pound pheasant
- 1 blood orange, chopped roughly
- Thyme
- Salt and pepper
- 4 slices of applewood smoked bacon

For the Cumberland sauce:
- 1/2 cup of calvados, brandy, cognac, bourbon or other brown liquor
- Juice of 1 blood orange
- 1 teaspoon of orange zest, minced
- 2/3 cup of red currant jelly
- Pinch of cayenne pepper
- Salt and pepper

Preheat the oven to 350°F.

Stuff the pheasant with the blood orange and thyme, and truss. Put the bird in the roasting pan, breast side up, and then layer the breasts with bacon. Put in the oven and roast for 1 hour and 15 minutes (should take about 20 to 25 minutes/pound until internal temperature is 165°F). Remove from the oven and begin making the sauce.

In a small saucepan, add calvados, orange juice, and zest. Heat on medium temperature for 5 minutes until the alcohol seems evaporated. Add the jelly, cayenne pepper, salt and pepper. Cook until nice and thick for another minute or two, at which point the sauce is ready. Put the sauce in a gravy boat and pour over the pheasant.

Serves 2.

Goat Kebabs [Main Course]

- 1 pound of goat meat in 1 inch cubes
- 1 teaspoon of cumin, ground
- 1/2 teaspoon of cinnamon, ground
- 1/4 teaspoon of cardamom, ground
- 1 clove of garlic, minced
- 1 small hot pepper, minced
- 6 ounces of yogurt
- Salt and pepper

Make a marinade by mixing the cumin, cinnamon, garlic and hot pepper, salt and pepper in the yogurt. Add the goat meat and marinate in the refrigerator for at least 2 hours or overnight.

Soak some wood skewers in water for 20 minutes, or use metal skewers.

Take the meat out of the marinade, flick off the liquid, and put on the skewers. Discard the marinade.

Grill or broil for about 7 to 10 minutes until done, flipping at least once.

Serves 2.

Pomes

Apple
- **Origin and cultivation:** was one of the first fruits to be cultivated, and the wild ancestor still grows in Kazakhstan
- **Availability:** becoming more and popular at farmers markets and gourmet grocery stores
- **Appearance:** green, red, deep burgundy or spotty
- **Flavor:** acidic crisp heirloom apples are great for cooking as well as eating out of hand
- **Trivia:** Golden Russet was discovered in New York in the mid-1800s and has a distinctive flavor resembling a sauvignon blanc, with a curious crispy texture; Newtown Pippin was discovered in what is now Queens in New York City in the early 1700s, was made famous by Thomas Jefferson, and is sweet, tart with a classic apple flavor; Northern Spy was discovered in New York in the early 1800s and is sweet, tart, juicy and holds up well when cooking making it the classic apple for pie; Winesap was discovered in the early 1800s in New Jersey and is very crisp, sweet and tart with a unique wine-like spicy flavor

Quince
- **Origin and cultivation:** was probably first cultivated in Persia or the Caucuses and was especially popular among the ancient Greeks and Romans
- **Availability:** fall
- **Appearance:** green fruit that looks like half apple half pear
- **Flavor:** has an intense floral delicious smell, and a quince left out in a room will fill the space with a pleasant fragrance
- **Trivia:** generally too astringent to eat raw so they are typically cooked with added sugar; because quinces have a lot of pectin, they keep their shape when cooked. Fell out of favor in the U.S. last century, but are making a comeback because of their unique flavor

Loquat
- **Also known as:** Biwa, Pipa, Nespole or Nispero
- **Origin and cultivation:** indigenous to China and popular in Asia
- **Availability:** bruise easily and don't travel well, so they are hard to find, but Asian markets and specialty groceries occasionally have them
- **Appearance:** small plumb-size fruit that varies in color from yellow to orange to apricot
- **Flavor:** have a nice sweet fruity flavor balanced with acidity
- **Trivia:** like other pomes, the seeds are slightly poisonous because they can release cyanide when digested

Asian Pear
- **Also known as:** Nashi Pear, Sand Pear, Apple Pear, Korean Pear, Japanese Pear or Chinese Pear
- **Origin and cultivation:** cultivated in Asia, gaining in popularity in the rest of the world
- **Availability:** year-round
- **Appearance:** pale yellow apple
- **Flavor:** sweet with a crispy crunchy texture
- **Trivia:** unlike other types of pears, the texture never softens as it ripens

www.newfoodcookbook.com

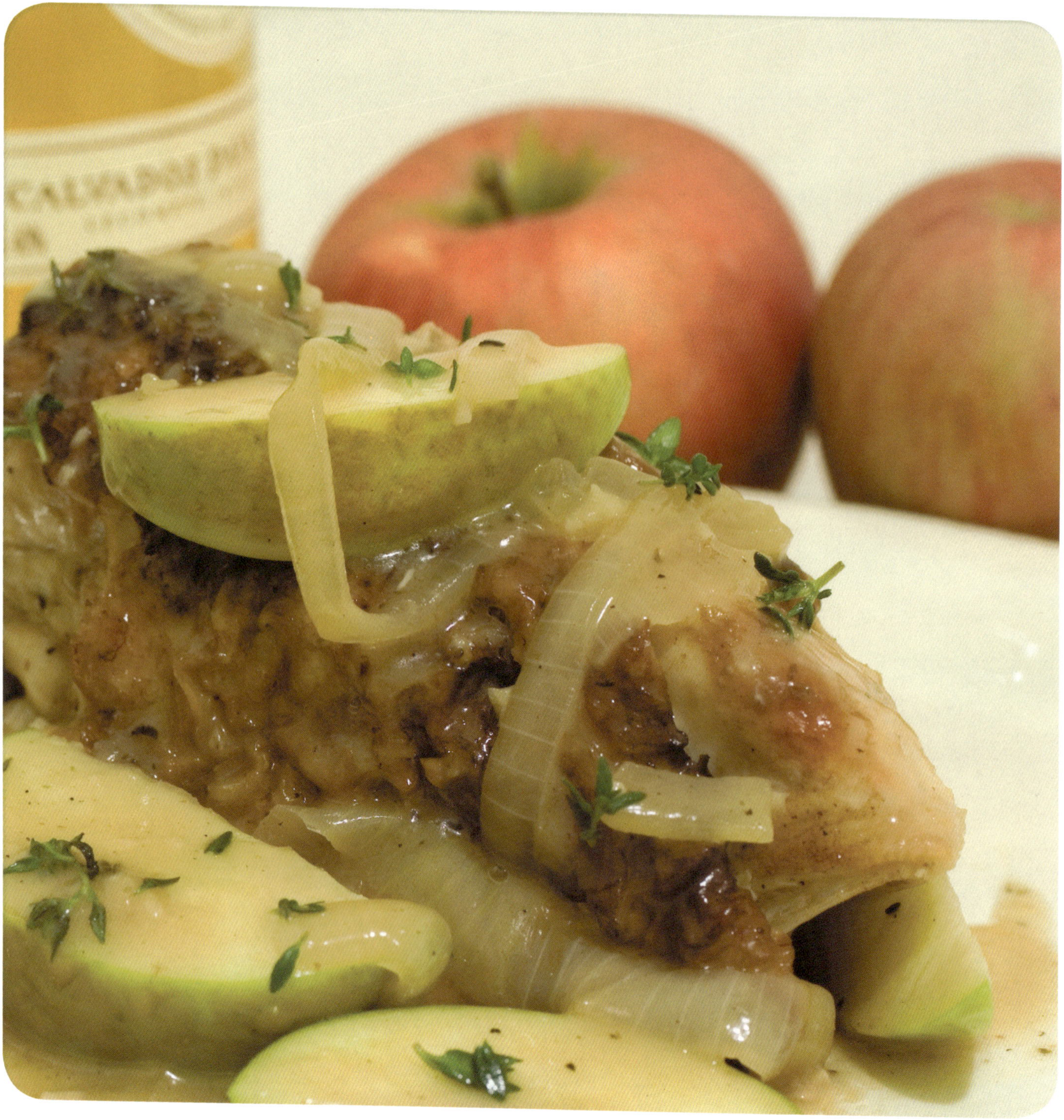

Apple Poached Chicken [Main Course]

- 4 chicken breasts
- 2 heirloom apples (a nice tart one such as a Golden Russet, Newtown Pippin, Northern Spy or Winesap)
- 1/2 cup of calvados
- 2 cups of apple cider
- 1 cup of chicken stock
- 2 tablespoons of butter
- 2 onions, sliced
- 1 clove of garlic, minced
- 1 teaspoon of fresh thyme leaves
- 2 teaspoons of corn starch dissolved in 1 tablespoon of cold water
- 1/4 cup of crème fraîche

Make sure the chicken is dry by blotting with a paper towel.

In a pot that you can eventually cover, heat butter over medium-high heat. Once hot, stick in the chicken skin side down and cook for 5 minutes without fidgeting with it. Then flip and cook another 3 minutes.

Remove the chicken and in the same pan, add the onion, garlic, salt and pepper. Cook for 2 minutes, then add the calvados, scrape up the brown bits stuck to the bottom and reduce until almost no liquid is left. Then, add the apple cider, chicken stock and thyme, bring to a boil and put the chicken breasts along with any accumulated juices back in the pan. If the chicken isn't completely covered in liquid, add another cup of apple cider, stock or water. Cover the pot and simmer on low for 25 minutes, flipping once, until the chicken is cooked through (internal temperature of 165°F).

Remove chicken and add the crème fraîche along with the corn starch dissolved in water. Cook on medium for about 7 minutes to reduce the sauce until it is nice and thick. While the sauce is reducing, core, peel and slice the apple, then toss the pieces into the sauce and remove from heat. Stir well and pour over chicken.

Serves 4.

Asian Pear Endive Salad [Starter]

- 2 endives
- 1 Asian pear
- 2 tablespoons of pine nuts
- 2 tablespoons of rice wine vinegar
- 1/3 cup of extra virgin olive oil
- 1 teaspoon of powdered mustard
- 1 hollowed out can
- Salt and pepper

First, toast the pine nuts in a toaster oven or a small pan for a minute or two until the aroma is enhanced.

Make a vinaigrette by whisking the vinegar, olive oil, mustard, salt and pepper.

Chop up the endives.

Core the pear and slice into thin rings. Use the hollowed out can to cut each pear slice into a perfect circle. Gently mix the endive and pears and pine nuts and vinaigrette, reserving a few pine nuts as garnish.

Then, use the same hollowed can as a mold on each plate, alternating layers of pear and spoonfuls of endive. Use a spoon to hold the salad steady and remove the can, leaving a nice stack. Garnish with pine nuts.

Serves 2.

Pan Roasted Pork Tenderloin with Quince [Main Course]

- 1 pork tenderloin (3/4 pound)
- 1 quince, cored, peeled, cut into eights
- 1 tablespoon of olive oil
- 1 tablespoon of butter
- 1/2 cup of apple cider
- 1/4 cup of demi-glace
- 1 teaspoon of fresh thyme
- Salt and pepper

Preheat your oven to 400°F. Sprinkle salt and pepper over the pork.

In an ovenproof pan on high heat, add the butter and olive oil. Sear the tenderloin on all sides for a few minutes. Add the quince. Put the pan in the oven and roast for about 20 minutes, turning the quince pieces over once until the internal temperature is 160°F.

Remove the pan from the oven and remove the pork, keeping it warm. With the quince pieces still in the pan, discard the grease, put it back on medium heat and add the apple cider, demi-glace and thyme. Stir and reduce for about 5 minutes until it is almost syrupy. Add salt and pepper.

Slice the pork and arrange the quince pieces around it. Pour the sauce.

Serves 2.

POMES

PAPPLEQUATINCE [Dessert]

A Papplequatince is a pear stuffed with an apple stuffed with a loquat stuffed with a quince.

- 1 pear
- 1 apple, the largest softball sized heirloom apple you can find, perhaps a Northern Spy which can grow quite large
- 1 quince
- 1 loquat
- 2 tablespoons of rolled oats
- 1 tablespoon of all purpose flour
- 1 tablespoon of cinnamon
- 2 tablespoons of butter, cold
- Pinch of salt

Preheat the oven to 350°F.

Mix the rolled oats, flour, brown sugar and cinnamon. Cut the butter into little pieces and use your hands to work it into the oat mixture.

Cut the top off the apple and use a melon baller to scoop out most of the inside, leaving the apple walls at least 1/4 inch thick.

Use an apple corer to gently core both sides of the loquat, using your fingers to push out the seeds.

Peel the quince, and cut in half top to bottom. Remove the inner core with a melon baller. Cut one nice long piece of quince that is about 1/2 inch thick and 4 inches long. Quince has a lot of pectin and will hold its shape during cooking so this piece will be used as the structural rebar.

Cut the pear in half, use the melon baller to scoop out some of the center so the hole is around 1/2 inch and will snuggly fit the other end of the quince. You'll only use the top half.

Put the apple on a baking dish or pan.

Dust the quince with some of the oatmeal mixture, then stuff the quince in the loquat, so that half the quince is sticking out. Put some of the oatmeal mixture into the bottom and sides of the hollowed out apple, then put the loquat into the center. Mound the oatmeal mixture into the apple, filling any holes. Put the pear on top of the apple, fitting the hollowed out area of the pear on top of the quince.

Bake the papplequatince for 30 minutes. Let cool for 15 minutes, before serving.

Serves 2.

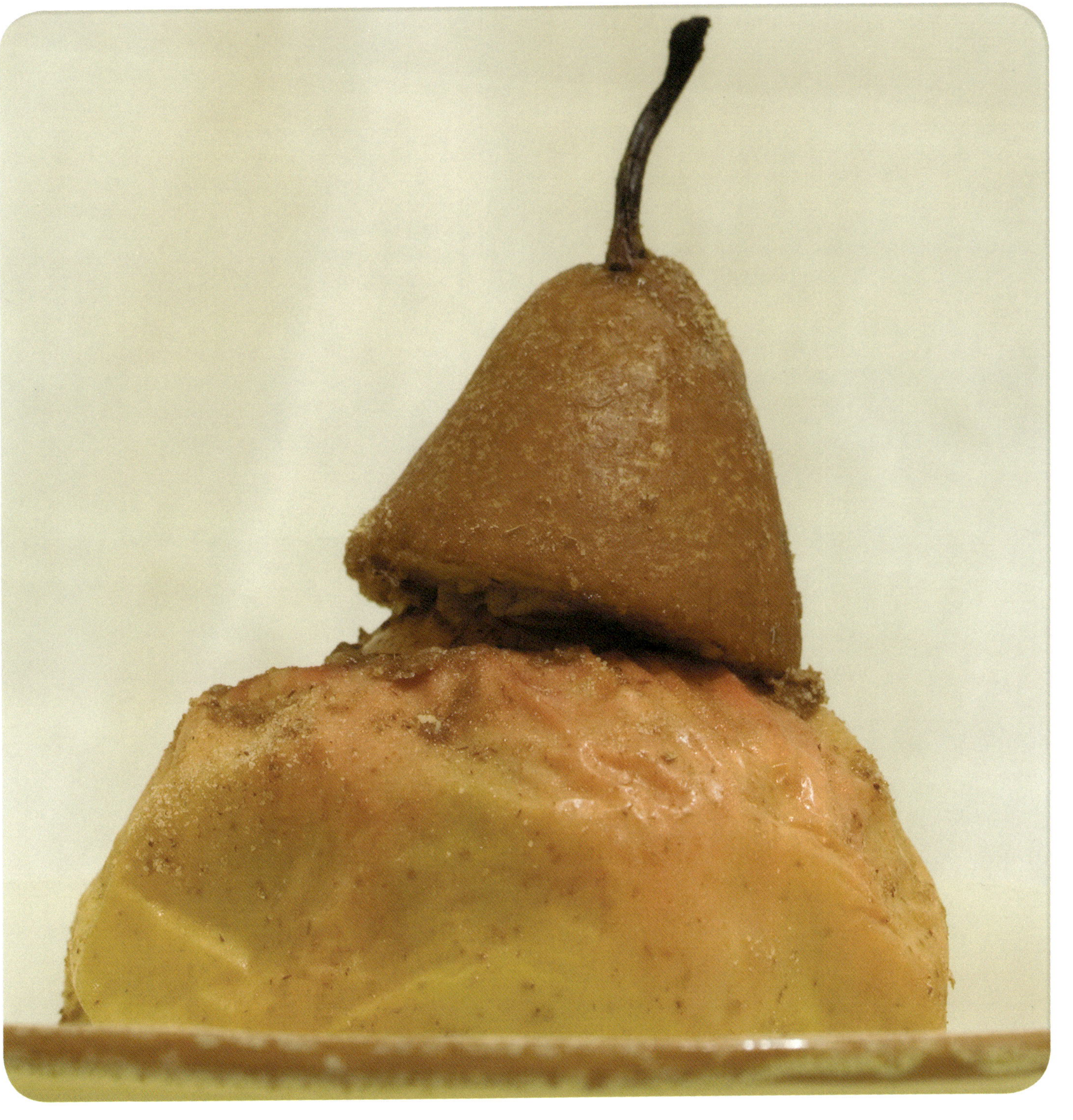

TURKEY BREAST WITH SPICY GINGER-QUINCE CHUTNEY [Main Course]

FOR THE TURKEY:
- 1 heritage turkey breast (about 3.5 lbs, including skin and bones and not split)
- 2 tablespoons of melted butter
- 2 tablespoons of fresh rosemary
- 1 shallot, minced
- Salt and pepper

FOR THE CHUTNEY:
2 quinces
1/4 cup of sugar
1/2 teaspoon of ground dried ginger
1 teaspoon of chardonnay vinegar
1/4 teaspoon of cayenne pepper
Dash of salt

Preheat the oven to 350°F.

Add half the rosemary to the melted butter and brush all over the turkey breast. Sprinkle on salt and pepper.

Put the turkey breast in a small roasting pan skin side up, and pour in 1 cup of water along with the shallot and remaining tablespoon of rosemary.

Roast for about 2 hours until the internal temperature is 180°F.

While the turkey is roasting, make the chutney. Peel the quinces, remove the core and seeds with a melon baller and chop into 1/2 inch pieces.

Put in the quince, sugar, ginger, vinegar, cayenne pepper and a dash of salt in a non-reactive saucepan (i.e. not aluminum). Bring to a boil, lower heat, cover and simmer for 35 minutes until it is nice and thick. Taste the chutney and if it is still too sour, add more sugar until the acid and sweet are balanced. Remove from heat and let it come to room temperature.

Carve up the turkey breast and serve with a dollop of chutney.

Serves 4.

Heirloom Apple Pie [Dessert]

For the pie crust:
- 2 cups of flour
- 1 teaspoon of salt
- 1 teaspoon of cinnamon
- 1 cup of unsalted butter
- 1/2 cup of ice water

For the filling:
- 3.5 pounds of heirloom apples (About 10 apples. Use a variety with some decent tartness such as Northern Spy, Rhode Island Greening, Newtown Pippin or Winesap)
- 2/3 cup brown sugar
- 3 tablespoons all-purpose flour
- 1 1/2 tablespoons ground cinnamon
- Dash of salt
- 2 tablespoons of butter

First, make your pie dough. The secret to good pie dough is to keep the butter cold. So, to make the pie dough, cut the butter into 1/2 inch pieces and stick in the freezer for 10 minutes.

Using a food processor with the metal cutting blade, add the flour, teaspoon of cinnamon and salt and pulse a couple of times. Then, add the butter and pulse on and off for 30 seconds scraping the sides to make sure everything gets mixed up. Slowly sprinkle the water on the flour, pulsing after each sprinkle to make the dough moist. If the dough is still too crumbly to roll into a ball, then add another dribble of water or two until you can form it.

Cut the dough in half and form into two thick discs. Cover each in cling wrap and refrigerate for 2 hours.

To make the pie filling, peel, core and slice the apples evenly into 1/3 inch slices. Put them in a bowl and add the brown sugar, 3 tablespoons of flour, dash of salt and ground cinnamon.

Put a wide pan on medium-low heat and add the 2 tablespoons of butter. Then add the apples. Cook for about 10 minutes, stirring very gently, to reduce their volume. Then, put the apples in a bowl and cool completely in the fridge.

After the dough and apples have chilled for 2 hours, preheat your oven to 425°F.

Roll one of the dough balls into about an 11 inch disk, and the other half to about 10 inches.

Put the larger dough disk into the pie pan, leaving a 1/2 inch overhang. Add the filling and put the rest of the pie dough on top and crimp. Cut 4 slices in the top for air vents.

Put the pie in the oven and bake for 20 minutes. Then, lower the heat to 375°F and continue baking for 35 more minutes or until the crust is golden. Remove from the oven and cool for at least 2 hours.

Serves 8.

Exotic Fruits

Horned Melon
- **Also known as:** Kiwano, African Horned Cucumber or Jelly Melon
- **Origin and cultivation:** originally from Africa, introduced to Australia and New Zealand in the early 20th century
- **Availability:** year-round
- **Appearance:** strange looking orange fruit with spikes, and has pulpy green gelatinous fruit inside
- **Flavor:** mild and reminiscent of cucumbers and kiwi
- **Trivia:** related to cucumbers and zucchini

Guava
- **Origin and cultivation:** native to South America
- **Availability:** year-round
- **Appearance:** large variety of skin and interior colors ranging from green to yellow to pink to red
- **Flavor:** nice balance of acidic and sweet with unique tropical flavors
- **Trivia:** related to myrtle

Açaí
- **Origin and cultivation:** native to the rain forest in Central and South America
- **Availability:** year-round in the freezer section, spoils quickly so is often found frozen
- **Appearance:** deep purple pulp
- **Flavor:** interesting and unique, with hints of chocolate and blueberry, is rich in fatty acids and has a fatty texture
- **Trivia:** popular in Brazil, especially among surfers and body builders who eat it for an energy boost

Pepino Melon
- **Also known as:** Mellowfruit, Treemelon, Melon Pear, Sweet Cucumber, Melon Shrub or Pear Melon
- **Origin and cultivation:** native to South America
- **Availability:** year-round
- **Appearance:** small oval melon
- **Flavor:** juicy with mild melon flavor
- **Trivia:** related to eggplant and potatoes, not other types of melons

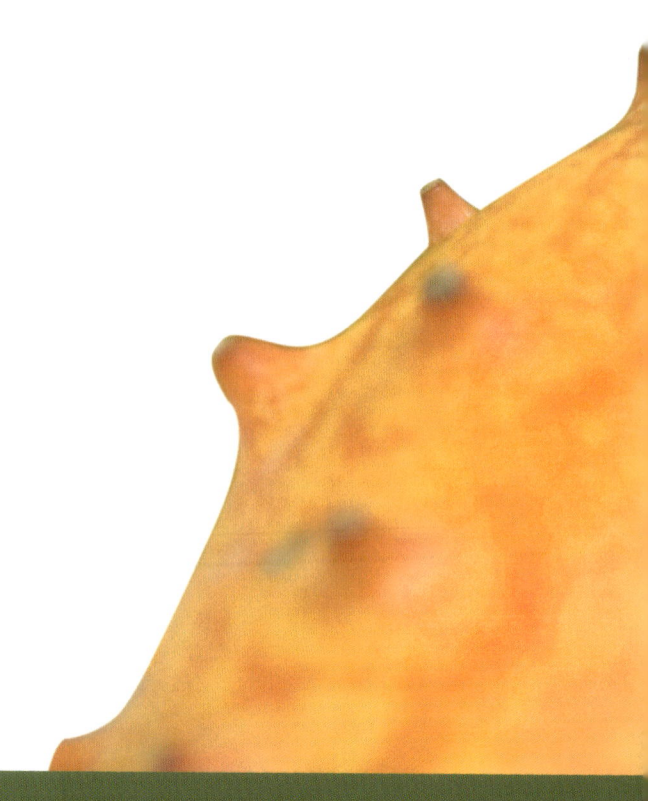

New Food – Contemporary recipes, fashionable ingredients

Cactus Pear
- **Also known as:** Prickly Pear, Tuna, Indian Fig, Indian Pear or Barbary Fig
- **Origin and cultivation:** Native to Mexico and surrounding regions
- **Availability:** year-round
- **Appearance:** color can range from green to yellow to magenta
- **Flavor:** resembles watermelon
- **Trivia:** some have inedible seeds, and others have soft seeds so be sure to check so you don't crack a tooth

Passion Fruit
- **Also known as:** as Granadilla
- **Origin and cultivation:** native to Brazil
- **Availability:** year-round
- **Appearance:** can be yellow or dark purple
- **Flavor:** sweet and tart, fruity
- **Trivia:** funny looking wrinkled rind means that it is ripe

www.newfoodcookbook.com

EXOTIC FRUITS

AÇAÍ SURFER BREAKFAST PARFAIT [Breakfast]

- 1/2 cup of Açaí frozen pulp
- 1 cup of granola
- 6 ounces of yogurt
- 2 parfait glasses

Defrost the frozen Açaí by leaving out of the freezer for 10 minutes. While it is still in the bag, you can smoosh it up with your hands to speed the defrosting process along.

Put alternating layers of Açaí, granola and yogurt in parfait glasses.

Serves 2.

HORNY BELLINI COCKTAIL [Cocktail]

- 1 horned melon
- Bottle of Prosecco sparkling wine, chilled

Cut about 1 inch off the end of the horned melon and cut in half. These pieces can be used for the garnish.

Then, cut the rest of the horned melon lengthwise into a few segments, and scoop out the seeds and juice into a cup. Refrigerate for 20 minutes to get them cold.

Add a few tablespoons of the seeds and juice to the bottom of a tall glass. Top off with Prosecco. Garnish with the reserved segments.

Serves 4.

EXOTIC FRUITS

GUAVA ON ENDIVE WITH GOAT CHEESE AND PINE NUTS [Starter]

- 2 endives
- 5 guava
- 2 tablespoons of goat cheese
- 2 tablespoons of pine nuts

On a big plate arrange the endive leaves in a fan pattern putting half a guava in the middle as a garnish. Put a 1/4 teaspoon of guava in each leaf. Then, sprinkle on the goat cheese and pine nuts.

Serves 4.

Cut the endive leaves off the head and keep them whole.

If you like, toast the pine nuts in a toaster oven or a small pan for a minute or two until the aroma is enhanced.

Scoop out the fruit from the guavas and reserve one half-piece to use as a garnish. Mash it up.

Crumble the goat cheese.

www.newfoodcookbook.com

HERITAGE MEATS & FARM RAISED GAME

PEPINO PROSCIUTTO PANINI [Main Course]

- 1 pepino melon
- 1/2 pound of Prosciutto di Parma
- 2 handfuls of arugula
- 1 loaf of ciabatta bread
- 2 tablespoons of olive oil

Peel the skin off the melon using a sharp knife and cut in half. Scoop out seeds and slice thinly.

Cut the bread into 4 pieces then slice each piece in half.

Create sandwiches by layering the melon, prosciutto and arugula in between the bread slices. Brush the outside of the bread with olive oil and grill in a pan or panini grill.

Serves 4.

PAN ROASTED MAHI MAHI WITH PASSION FRUIT [Main Course]

- 2 Mahi Mahi filets (1 pound total)
- 1/2 of a Vidalia onion, sliced
- 3 passion fruits
- 1 tablespoon of soy sauce
- 1 teaspoon of ginger, minced
- 2 tablespoons of butter

Cut the passion fruits in half and scoop out the fruit inside, keeping in a bowl for the time being. Discard the passion fruit rinds.

Put a nice heavy pan on medium heat and add 1 tablespoon of butter. Once hot, add the Mahi Mahi filets and cook for 3 minutes/side. Remove and keep warm.

In the same pan, add the remaining tablespoon of butter, and cook the onion and ginger for 5 minutes until it begins to caramelize. Turn off the heat, and deglaze the pan by splashing in the soy sauce and passion fruit and stirring gently with a spoon. Pour the sauce on the fish.

Serves 2.

Lamb Chops with Cactus Pear Sauce [Main Course]

- 1/2 rack of lamb (8 ribs)
- 1 cactus pear
- 3 cloves of garlic, minced
- 1 tablespoon of freshly chopped mint
- 1/4 cup of dry white wine
- 1 shallot, minced
- 1 tablespoon of butter
- 1 tablespoon of olive oil
- Salt and pepper

Cut the lamb chops into 2 pieces of 4 ribs each.

Preheat the oven to 425°F.

Mince the garlic until it is nearly liquefied, using a fine grater. Add mint, olive oil, salt and pepper to the garlic. Smear over the 2 pieces of lamb chops.

Balance the chops on each other, put in an ovenproof pan, and then roast for about 25 minutes until the internal temperature of the lamb reaches 160°F.

While the lamb is roasting, peel the cactus pear: Using a small knife, score cactus lengthwise 4 or 5 times, then peel off strips of the skin. If the seeds are soft and edible, coarsely chop. If the seeds are hard, put chucks of the cactus pear in a metal mesh strainer and squish the pulp through, discarding the seeds.

Once the lamb is done, remove from the pan and keep warm. Pour out some of the grease.

Put the pan on medium heat and add the shallot. Cook for about 2 or 3 minutes then add the cactus pear, white wine, salt and pepper. Stir in the brown bits stuck on the bottom with a spoon. Reduce the sauce for 4 or 5 minutes then remove from heat.

Cut up the lamb chops and spoon the sauce on top.

Serves 2.

Heirloom Tomatoes

Heirloom Tomatoes

- **Origin and cultivation:** tomatoes are a New World fruit, native to the Americas; generally understood to be any tomato that isn't red, smooth and round; they are sometimes defined as varieties that are over 100 years old, pre-WWII, or by other dates
- **Availability:** summer at farmers markets and increasingly, year-round at grocery stores as some heirloom varieties are being grown on a larger commercial scale
- **Appearance:** colors range from green to yellow to orange to dark burgundy to purple to brown; tend to be open pollinated causing a lot of variety; grape, cherry and pear tomatoes in different colors beyond red are becoming increasingly common
- **Flavor:** like great tomatoes
- **Trivia:** when first brought to Europe, people considered them poisonous

www.newfoodcookbook.com

Heirloom Tomatoes

Heirloom Tomato Tabouli Salad [Starter]

- 1 cup of bulgur
- 2 cups of boiling water
- 3 heirloom tomatoes, each a different color
- 1 cucumber
- 2 scallions
- 1 cup of parsley, minced
- Juice of 1 lemon
- 3 tablespoons of extra virgin olive oil
- Salt and pepper

First, you need to soak the bulgur: Pour the 2 cups of boiling water over the bulgur, cover and let sit for 1 hour or until light and fluffy. Then, drain any excess water.

Remove the seeds of the tomatoes, and then chop. Peel and remove the seeds from the cucumber and chop. Chop the scallions. Add the lemon juice, olive oil, salt and pepper to the bulgur and mix. Refrigerate until needed. This is a good salad to make a day ahead of time.

Serves 4.

Heirloom Tomato Goat Cheese Toasts [Starter]

- 1 baguette
- 8 heirloom tomatoes, various colors
- 4 ounces of goat cheese
- 2 tablespoons of julienned purple basil

Slice the baguette into diagonal pieces.

Slice the tomatoes.

On each baguette piece, put a layer of tomatoes. Then, crumble the goat cheese on top.

Put under the broiler for 5 to 6 minutes or until crispy. Remove, and sprinkle with the basil.

Serves 4.

WILD STRIPED BASS WITH HEIRLOOM CHERRY TOMATOES IN PAPER [Main Course]

HEIRLOOM TOMATOES

- 2 wild striped bass filets, 6 ounces each (red snapper is another alternative)
- 1 cup of multi-colored heirloom cherry and grape tomatoes
- 10 big green Cerignola olives, whole
- 1 teaspoon of capers, rinsed
- 1 cup of couscous
- 2 teaspoons of Provençal herbs (herb mix including thyme, tarragon, lavender, and/or rosemary)
- 1/2 cup of dry white wine
- Juice of 1 lemon
- 2 tablespoons olive oil
- Parchment paper
- Salt and pepper

Preheat your oven to 425°F.

You will make each filet separately in its own parchment paper.

First, take the couscous and put in a bowl. Add the white wine, herbs, olive oil, salt and pepper, and then gently mix.

Tear off a 2 foot long piece of parchment paper.

On one piece of paper, put a piece of fish in the middle, and then pile half of the couscous around it. Next, scatter half the capers, olives, and tomatoes on the fish. Then sprinkle lemon juice over everything.

Seal the paper as if wrapping a piece of hard candy: take the longer ends of the paper and bring to the middle, then fold over 5 or 6 times. Then, twist the ends shut.

Repeat the whole process with the second filet.

Put the fish packages on a baking sheet, then into the oven. Roast for 18 minutes at 425°F.

Once done, carefully put the paper package on a plate. Make sure that when you and your guest cut open the paper, everyone is watching the dramatic release of steam.

Serves 2.

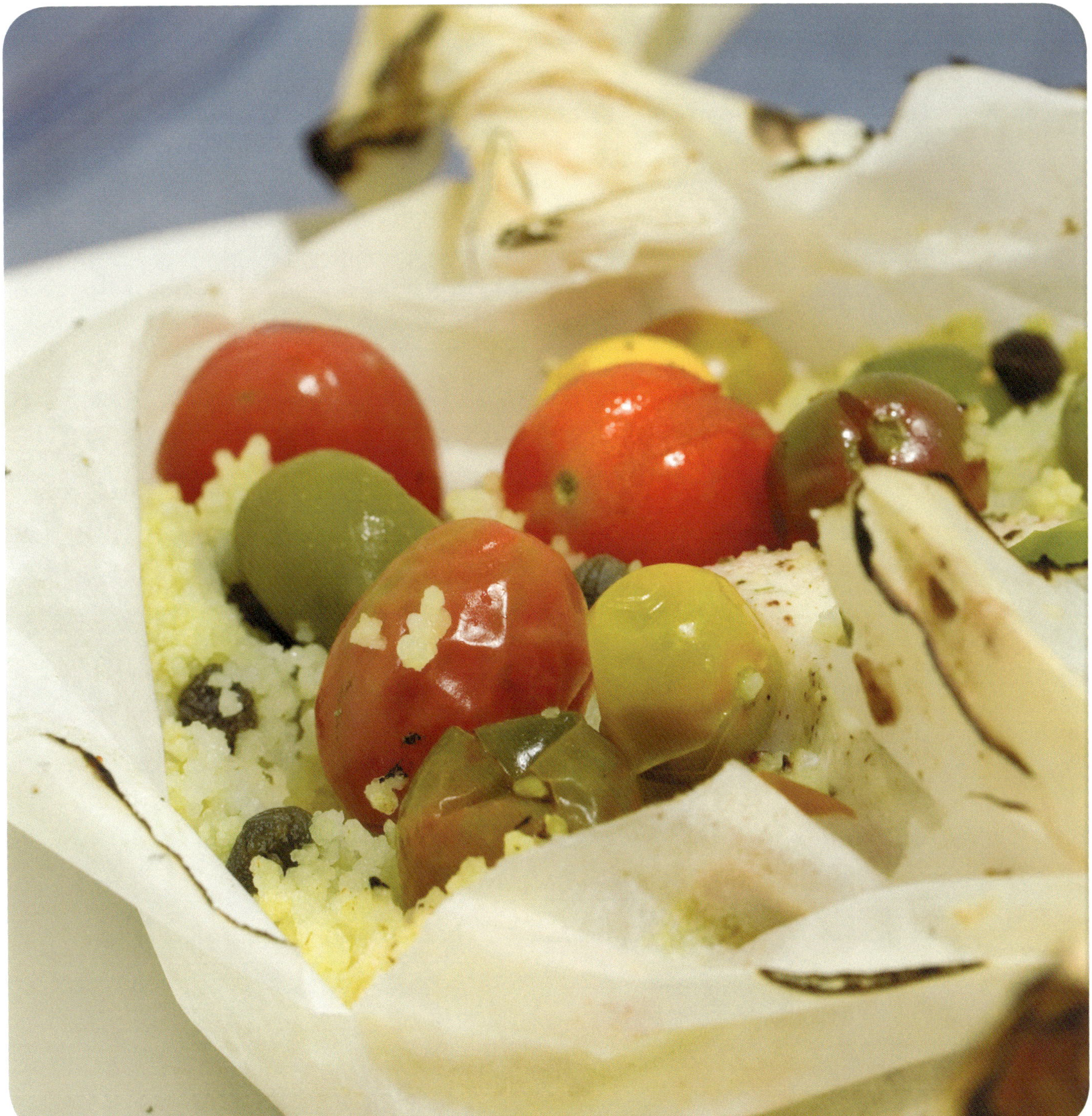

Heirloom Tomatoes

Chorizo with Colored Grape Tomatoes and Saffron Rice [Main Course]

- 4 chorizo sausages (about 2/3 of a pound)
- 2 cups of multi-colored heirloom grape tomatoes
- 2 tablespoons of olive oil
- 1 tablespoon of fresh mint, chopped
- 1 cup of basmati rice
- 1 pinch of saffron
- Salt and pepper

Rinse the rice until the water runs clear and soak in water for 10 minutes.

Strain your rice after 10 minutes of soaking. In a pot, add 1 1/2 cup of water, saffron, 1 tablespoon of olive oil and a pinch of salt and bring to a boil. Add the rice to the pot, stir once, cover and lower heat to as low as possible. Cook the rice for 15 minutes, and then turn off the heat allowing the covered rice to steam an additional 5 minutes.

While the rice is cooking, slice the chorizo into 1/2 inch slices, slightly diagonally.

Put a pan on medium-high heat and add the olive oil. Once hot, add the chorizo and fry for 2 minutes, the flip and fry another 2 minutes so that they look nice and brown. Add the grape tomatoes and stir. Cook for another 4 minutes, stirring occasionally. Remove from heat and add the mint.

Put the rice on a plate alongside the chorizo and tomatoes.

Serves 2.

Heirloom Tomato Mozzarella Basil Orecchiette [Main Course]

- 6 different colored heirloom tomatoes
- 3 tablespoons of fresh basil, chopped
- 1 pound of orcchiette shaped pasta
- 8 ounces of fresh mozzarella (about 1 ball)
- 2 tablespoons of extra virgin olive oil
- Salt and pepper

Boil and drain the pasta.

Mix the pasta with the tomatoes, mozzarella, basil, olive oil, salt and pepper. You can serve hot or cold.

Serves 4.

Peel the tomatoes by boiling them in water for 1 minute. Remove and dunk in an ice bath to cool them down and peel.

Then, slice the tomatoes in half and remove the seeds. Chop the tomatoes into 1/4 inch pieces.

Chop the mozzarella into 1/4 inch pieces.

Ancient Grains

Bhutanese Red Rice
- **Origin and cultivation:** grown in Bhutan in the Himalayas
- **Availability:** year-round
- **Appearance:** red color is from tannin pigments
- **Flavor:** like rice
- **Trivia:** staple food of people living in Bhutan

Black Rice
- **Also known as:** Black Sticky Rice, Black Glutinous Rice
- **Origin and cultivation:** grown across Asia
- **Availability:** year-round
- **Appearance:** dark purple color is primarily from anthocyanin pigments
- **Flavor:** like rice
- **Trivia:** one variety is known as forbidden rice because legend says it was once consumed only by Chinese royalty and their concubines; traditionally used in sweet dessert or breakfast dishes

Bulgur
- **Also known as:** Bulgar, Burghul, Bulgur Wheat or Ali
- **Origin and cultivation:** made from soaked wheat that has been baked dry (by an oven or the sun) then cracked
- **Availability:** year-round
- **Appearance:** little brown rough granules
- **Flavor:** mild wheat flavor
- **Trivia:** considered man's first processed food, first prepared over 4,000 years ago

Quinoa
- **Origin and cultivation:** from the Andes where it has been an important food for over 5,000 years;
- **Availability:** year-round
- **Appearance:** comes in different colors ranging from tan to red to black
- **Flavor:** seeds have a bitter coating of saponins which are typically removed during commercial processing, so check the instructions on your package of quinoa to make sure it was pre-rinsed
- **Trivia:** staple food of the Incas; not a true grain, but actually a seed so it is known as a pseudo-cereal

Amaranth
- **Origin and cultivation:** grown by the Aztecs over 5,000 years ago
- **Availability:** year-round
- **Appearance:** tiny round tan grains
- **Flavor:** mild and nutty
- **Trivia:** it was incorporated in ancient images of gods and consumed in religious ceremonies which, to the Europeans, resembled a pagan parody of Christian communion leading them to ban it

www.newfoodcookbook.com

93

Ancient Grains

Quinoa Granola [Breakfast]

- 3 cups of quinoa
- 3 cups of rolled oats
- 1 cup of sliced almonds
- 1/2 cup of maple syrup
- 1/2 cup of hazelnut oil
- 1 tablespoon of cinnamon
- 1 vanilla bean
- Pinch of salt

Preheat the oven to 350°F.

Follow the directions on the box or bag of quinoa to see if rinsing is necessary, and if so, rinse the quinoa and drain. If pre-rinsed, then it is ready to be used.

Scrape out the vanilla bean seeds.

In a decent sized bowl, stir the maple syrup and hazelnut oil together. Scrape out the seeds from the vanilla bean and add them to the bowl. Also, add the cinnamon and pinch of salt. Mix well so everything is dispersed. Then, add the quinoa, oats and almonds.

Spread the mixture on a baking sheet and cook for 25 to 30 minutes, stirring every 7 minutes or so until evenly toasted. Be careful not to let it burn.

Cool, and store in an airtight container. It should last for a couple of weeks.

Serves 8.

Lamb Mushroom Bulgur Soup [Starter]

- 2 lbs of leg of lamb cut into small pieces (1/2 to 1 inch)
- 1 medium onion, chopped
- 6 carrots, roughly chopped
- 7 sticks of celery, roughly chopped
- 1 cup of white fresh mushrooms, sliced
- 1 tablespoon of butter
- 2 quarts of beef or lamb stock
- 2/3 cup of bulgur
- 1 bouquet garni (a bay leaf, sprig of fresh thyme and sprig of rosemary tied together)

In a large 4 or 5 quart heavy pot, sauté the onions, carrots and celery in the butter for 3 minutes.

Add the lamb and cook 4 more minutes.

Add the mushrooms and cook 3 more minutes.

Add the beef stock and bouqet garni. As it comes to a boil, skim off the foam.

Cover and simmer for 1 hour until the lamb is tender. Then, add the bulgur, put the cover back on and simmer for another ten minutes. If there is excessive fat on the top, skim some off. Discard the bouquet garni.

Serves 6.

Ancient Grain and Rice Pilaf [Side Dish]

- 1 1/2 cup of basmati rice
- 1/2 cup of whole ancient grains such as amaranth, ragi, red rice or quinoa
- 3 1/2 cups of chicken stock
- 1/2 cup of sliced almonds
- 1 leek, cleaned well and chopped
- 2 cloves of garlic, minced
- 1/2 teaspoon of fresh sage
- 1/2 teaspoon of fresh thyme
- 2 tablespoons of olive
- Salt and pepper

Put the rice and grains together in a bowl, and rinse a few times with cold water until the water runs clear. Drain.

In a small pot, on medium-high heat, add the olive oil. Once hot, add the leek, garlic and almonds. Cook for 2 minutes, add the stock and bring to a boil.

Add the drained rice and grains to the boiling pot, along with the sage, thyme, salt and pepper. Lower the heat and cover tightly. Simmer for 20 minutes.

Fluff with a fork before serving.

Serves 4.

ANCIENT GRAINS

BLACK RICE PUDDING [Dessert]

- 1 cup of black glutinous rice
- 1/4 cup of maple syrup
- 1 cup of coconut milk
- 1 teaspoon of cinnamon
- Pinch of salt

Bring 3 cups of water with a pinch of salt to a boil. Add the rice, cover, then simmer for about 30 minutes. Add the syrup, coconut milk and cinnamon and simmer for 20 more minutes uncovered, stirring occasionally until nice and thick.

Serve at room temperature or chilled.

Serves 4.

BHUTANESE RED CHESTNUT RICE [Side Dish]

- 6 fresh chestnuts
- 1 cup of red rice
- 1 tablespoon of butter
- Salt

Carefully cut an X in each chestnut with a knife. Microwave all 6 chestnuts for about 35 seconds. Let cool for at least 5 minutes and peel off the shells.

Bring 1 1/2 cup of water to a boil. Add the rice, chestnuts, butter and salt. Bring to a boil, cover and simmer on the lowest heat for 25 minutes. Remove from heat and let sit covered for another 5 minutes.

Gently fluff before serving which will break up chestnuts a little.

Serves 2.

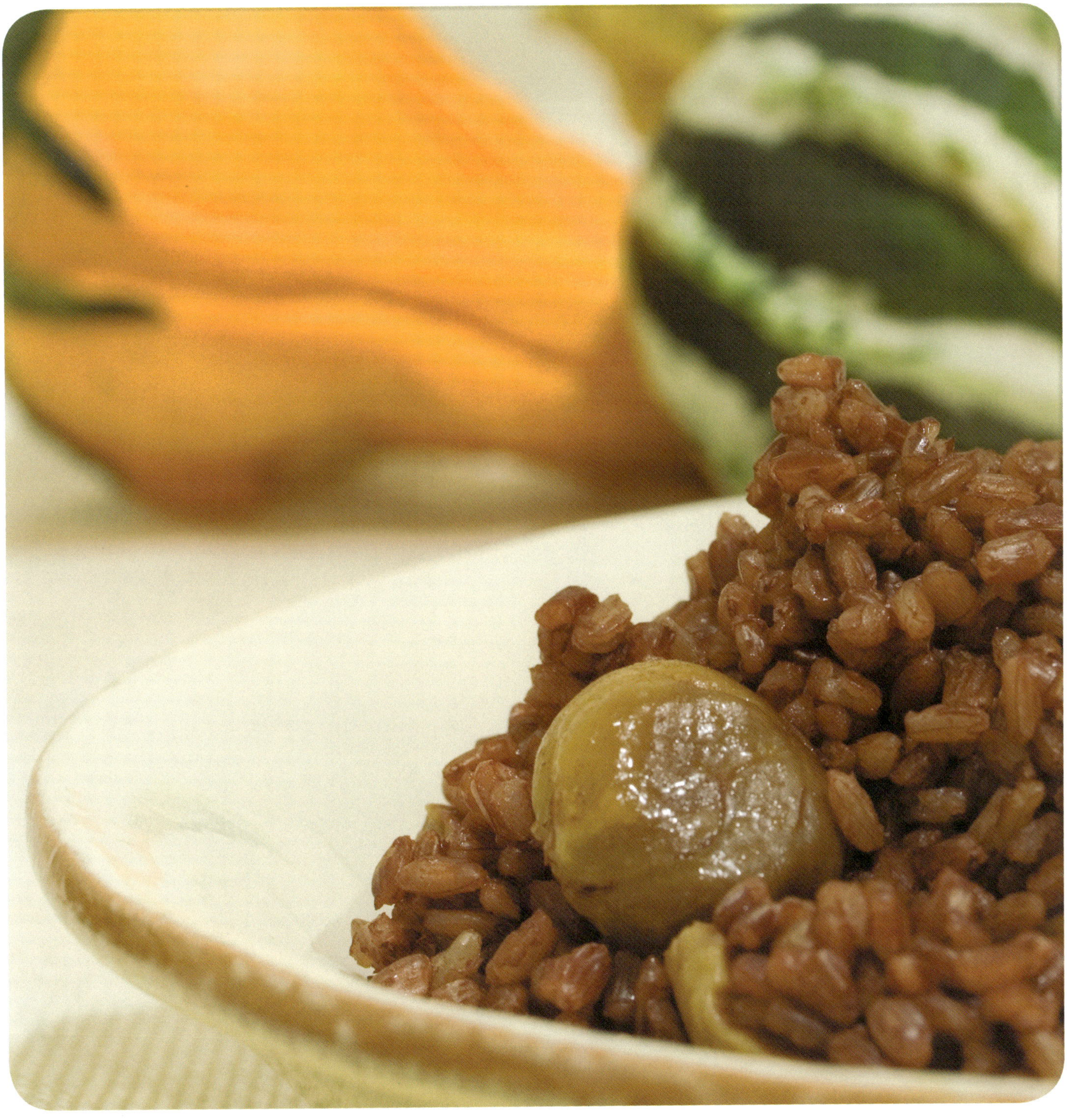

ANCIENT GRAINS

AMARANTH SALAD [Side Dish]

- 1/2 cup of whole grain amaranth
- 1/2 cup of corn
- 1 red bell pepper
- 1 yellow bell pepper
- 1 green bell pepper
- 1 small red onion, chopped
- 1 teaspoon of fresh sage, finely chopped
- 2 tablespoons of extra virgin olive oil
- Juice of 1 lemon
- Salt and pepper

Dice the bell peppers.

In a pan, on high heat, add the olive oil. Then, once hot, add the bell peppers, onion and corn. Sauté for about 5 minutes until the corn is cooked through. Toss with the cooked amaranth along with the fresh sage, lemon juice, salt and pepper. Refrigerate for at least 2 hours.

Serves 6.

Rinse and drain the amaranth grains. Combine amaranth with 1 1/4 cups of salted water and bring to a boil. Lower heat, cover and simmer for 25 minutes.

ABOUT THE AUTHOR
Ben Lewis is a food writer living in New York City with his wife and daughter.

Special thanks to Nari, Rodrigo, Paula K. and Sarah for their help with this book.

Printed in the United States
120309LV00001B